Sage Sterling

for Windows

Explained

OTHER TITLES OF INTEREST

Sage Sterling +2
for Windows
Explained

By

David Weale

BERNARD BABANI (publishing) LTD
THE GRAMPIANS
SHEPHERDS BUSH ROAD
LONDON W6 7NF
ENGLAND

PLEASE NOTE

First published - May 1995

British Library Cataloguing in Publication Data

Weale. D
Sage Sterling +2 for Windows Explained
I.Title
657.02855369

ISBN 0 85934 361 8

Printed and bound in Great Britain by Cox & Wyman Ltd., Reading.

ABOUT THE AUTHOR

David Weale is a Fellow of the Institute of Chartered Accountants and has worked in both private and public practice. At present he is a lecturer in business computing at Yeovil College.

Apart from computing his interests are running and cycling.

He lives in Somerset with his wife, three children and Siamese cat.

DEDICATION

This book is for all those who have pointed the way.

TRADEMARKS

MS-DOS is a registered trademark of Microsoft Corporation

SAGE Sterling +2 is a registered trademark of SAGE PLC.

Contents

Introduction

This book is intended to explain the uses and methodology of SAGE Sterling for Windows.

It is not supposed to be, in any way, a replacement or substitute for the manual that comes with the program but is a supplementary text which could help the user with understanding of the program.

It could be used by anyone having bought the program who wants a simple explanatory text or by someone thinking of buying the program who wants to see how it works.

For the purposes of this book it is assumed that the reader has the program installed on their computer and is familiar with the WINDOWS environment. If necessary there are many easy to follow books available for this purpose.

I hope you enjoy it.

David Weale

Common information

There are various symbols and buttons that are common to many parts of the program and these are explained here.

Using the scroll bars

Some of the dialog boxes have scroll bars, these have an arrow at the top and bottom and you click on the arrows to move up or down the list shown within the dialog box.

An example is shown below.

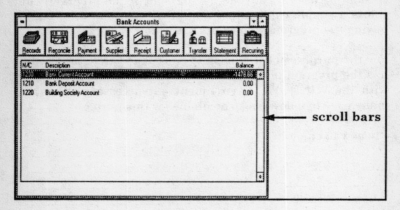

scroll bars

Scroll bars also appear along the bottom of some windows and dialog boxes.

Moving around the dialog boxes

Click the mouse pointer in the required box. Within each dialog box you can use either the mouse or you can TAB between each field.

To move up (or backwards) within the dialog box hold down the SHIFT key and then press the TAB key.

Selecting records

Many of the dialog boxes display a list of items, for example customer names or nominal codes. You can select any of these by clicking the mouse pointer on them.

To select more than one simply click again and you will see that both are highlighted (and so on if you want to select more).

To alter the selection you can deselect by clicking the mouse on the item again or you can use the available buttons (see the next page).

Useful function keys

There are several function keys used within the program, the most useful are as follows.

F1	Brings up the HELP screens
F2	Displays the calculator
F4	Displays a list of alternate choices e.g. A/C codes
F5	Inserts the current (system) date
F6	Deletes / resets the entry within some fields
F11	Loads the WINDOWS Control Panel
F12	Loads WINDOWS WRITE (to edit layouts)

Buttons

Windows Buttons

You can exit from the section you are using (or the program itself) by clicking on the symbol in the top left hand corner of the window and selecting CLOSE.

Clicking on this button reduces the window you are using to an icon, to enlarge the icon click on it and choose the relevant option from the menu shown (e.g. MAXIMISE will enlarge the window to full screen).

Clicking on this button makes the window full screen.

This reduces a full screen window to its previous size.

Dialog Buttons Within SAGE

 When you click on this button you will be presented with a list from which you can choose. This button appears within many of the dialog boxes in the program. It works in a similar way to the **F4** function key.

 Clicking on this produces a set of alternative choices. To choose one of these instead of the one already shown, scroll down the list and click on your choice. This button also appears within many of the dialog boxes in the program.

 Within some of the dialog boxes you can, if you wish, set criteria for your choice. For example you may choose only those customers owing more than a certain amount of money.

 This swaps the selection to the other (unselected) records.

 This clears the Criteria selection.

For an explanation of the various criteria see Appendix three.

The various dialog boxes within SAGE contain additional buttons, the following are common to most modules (although they do not all individually appear in all the dialog boxes).

Save

This enables you to save the current dialog box, for example a customer record.

Abandon

If you make a mess of the data entry or an alteration to a record then you can abandon it and start again.

Prev / Next

If you have selected all the records then these buttons let you move from the current one to the next or previous.

Delete

You can delete the current (record). There is usually another screen to check that you are certain you want to delete the item.

Memo

This lets you add suitable text to the item.

Close

When you want to return to the previous menu after having finished with the current screen.

Instant Help (v2.1 only)

Throughout the program there are explanations and hints which appear automatically when you leave the mouse pointer on a button or data entry field for a few seconds.

Two examples of these are shown below.

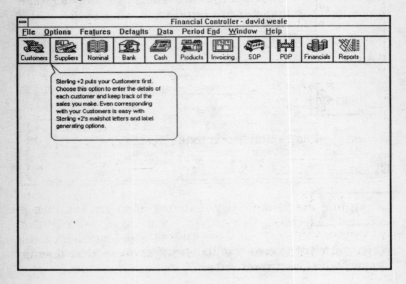

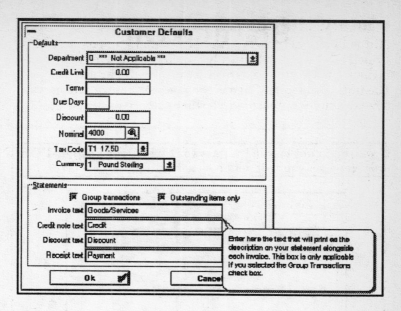

Customer Defaults

Defaults

Department	0 *** Not Applicable ***
Credit Limit	0.00
Terms	
Due Days	
Discount	0.00
Nominal	4000
Tax Code	T1 17.50
Currency	1 Pound Sterling

Statements

☒ Group transactions   ☒ Outstanding items only

Invoice text	Goods/Services
Credit note text	Credit
Discount text	Discount
Receipt text	Payment

Enter here the text that will print as the description on your statement alongside each invoice. This box is only applicable if you selected the Group Transactions check box.

Ok ✓   Cancel

If you find the Instant Help irritating, then you can turn it off by selecting DEFAULTS and then COMPANY PREFERENCES. Then select DEFAULTS and click on the TOOLBAR HELP and FIELD HELP boxes so that they do **not** have a cross.

You can still activate the Instant Help within data fields by clicking the **right hand** mouse button.

Starting Off

The initial screen for Sage is the password entry screen, you have to enter your password so that you are recognised as an acceptable user.

If you have not created a password when you installed the program then you will not be asked for a password.

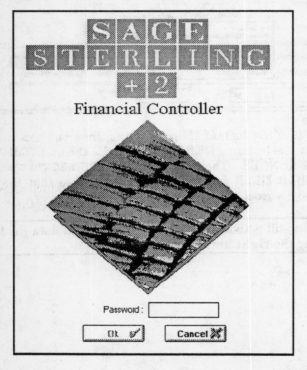

Your password is created when you originally install the program, you can also alter it at any time by selecting DEFAULTS and then COMPANY PREFERENCES.

Main Menu

After entering your password you will be presented with the following screen which is the MAIN MENU screen.

You select your option by clicking on your choice of icon.

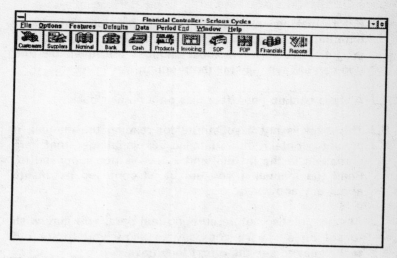

There are also several pull down menus which can be accessed by clicking on the command shown along the top of the screen.

Several Words Of Warning

❑ Before making any alteration to the program defaults or entering any data, you may like to make a backup of the program files however most changes are reversible and you can always reinstall the program.

❑ Always backup your data files on a regular basis.

❑ This book is not a substitute for reading the manual, it cannot contain the detailed explanations that are contained in the manual and indeed is not supposed to. Read the manual if you are at all confused or unsure about any activity.

❑ Always practise before entering real data, you may wish to set up a special company to allow you to try out techniques to see the effect they have.

❑ Do **not** enter data unless you are clear about what will happen to your accounts as a result of entering that data.

❑ Run parallel systems (manual and computer) until you are very confident that the computer system is functioning satisfactorily.

❑ Start with a small section of your accounts on the computer to gain confidence and experience, for example the sales ledger.

❑ Use your accountant's knowledge and skill to help you.

❑ Subscribe to the SAGE help line. It is very useful and worthwhile, you can phone for any help you need and will get information about upgrades and so on.

The Pull Down Menus

Along the top of the screen are several commands. Clicking on any of these gives rise to a (pull down) menu. From this list you select the command you want and so on.

Within each pull down menu you can select the command you want by clicking on it with the mouse or by moving the cursor onto it by using the cursor control keys and then pressing the RETURN key.

File menu
From this you have the following choices.

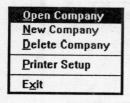

Open Company
This displays a list of the other companies you have set up within SAGE and you can select any of these by clicking on the required name and then on the OK button.

New Company

You can set up another company by using this option. You may run this company as a separate business or you can treat it as a subsidiary of the original company in which case you can consolidate it at the year end.

The data you can enter is shown below (V.2 has fewer items).

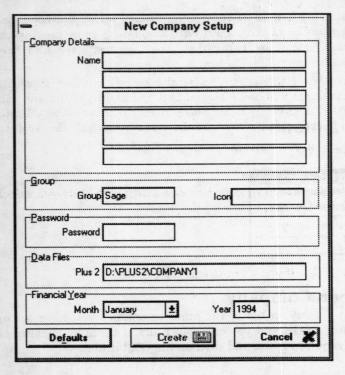

You must enter the directory you want the data files to be stored in. If the directory does not exist then SAGE will create it and you can choose which WINDOWS group you wish the company to be displayed in on the main WINDOWS screen by entering a group name in the GROUP box (it would, however, be normal to leave it in the SAGE group window).

Within this option you can alter the default settings for this company if you want them to be different to the original.

For details of Company Preference Defaults see the section on DEFAULTS.

Delete Company

A very powerful option, this enables you (or anyone with the password) to delete a subsidiary or additional company from the disc.

If you select this option a list of companies (other than the current one) will be displayed and you highlight the one you want to delete by clicking the mouse pointer and you will then be asked twice if you really want to do this. Be careful.

Printer Setup

If you have set up more than one printer this lets you select the one you want to use for the output.

Exit

Choose this if you want to exit from SAGE.

Options menu

The menu for this contains the following and is an alternative to the use of the buttons in selecting any of the modules making up the program (for example if you have turned off the toolbar displaying all the module icons).

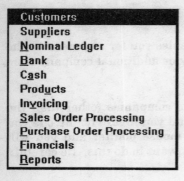

Features menu

This option contains three choices as shown below

The first three of these give rise to another menu and these will be dealt with within the specific module i.e. the CUSTOMER FEATURES will be dealt within the CUSTOMERS section, the SUPPLIER within the SUPPLIERS section and the INVOICE features within the INVOICING section.

The LOG OFF feature allows you to logout of the program without actually exiting from it. This would leave the program running so that another user could log in. This option is only available if you have used the ACCESS RIGHTS option within the DEFAULTS menu.

Defaults menu

These are the original settings that come with SAGE. You can alter them if you so wish and then your settings become the defaults.

The choice is shown below.

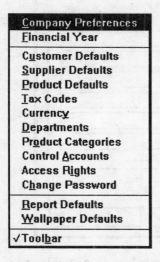

Each of these will be dealt with in sequence.

Company Preferences

These are set when you install the program or create a new company. As you can see from the illustration, the screen shows the name, address and password, any of which you can alter.

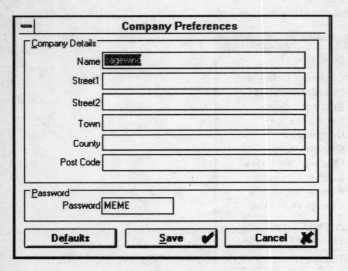

Note the button on the left of the dialog box, this enables you to alter the defaults shown below.

In v.2 of the program there are fewer options within this screen.

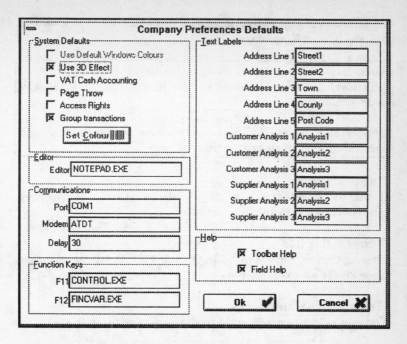

Use Default Windows Colours (Set Colour)
Many happy hours can be spent altering the colours that are show on the screen. You will be given a palette of colours which you can select as you wish.

This option cannot be used if you have selected 3D EFFECT.

VAT Cash Accounting
You can change the way VAT is accounted for, this is a very important decision as it will affect the completion of the VAT returns and consequently your VAT liability.

If you choose to select VAT Cash Accounting then you will be accounting for VAT only when invoices are paid or when you buy for cash or by cheque. (The standard method of accounting for VAT is to calculate your input and output tax on the basis of invoices and credit notes at the time you send or receive them).

To select VAT Cash Accounting (if you so decide) click on the box so that an X appears.

Notes:
It is essential that you discuss how to account for VAT with your accountant.

Once you have started to post invoices you cannot switch back from VAT cash accounting.

Page Throw
If this is selected a new page will be started for history reports for each individual account.

Access Rights
This option is only available in V.2.1 of the program, see page 26 for an explanation.

Group Transactions
You can select to group data of the same type together.

Function Keys
Unless these boxes contain the relevant program they will not function as expected. You can, of course, alter the programs that they will automatically load if you so wish.

Financial Year
You can alter the start of the financial year within this, but only if you have not posted any data.

Customer Defaults

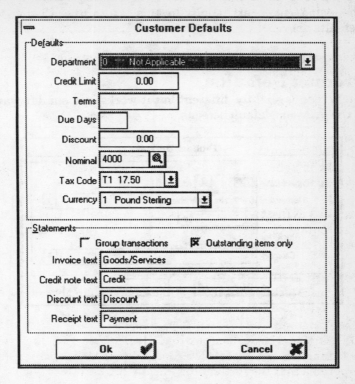

Selecting this allow you to alter the default settings for customers.

You can alter any of these and they will appear automatically on every customer account you set up, you can obviously change them on an individual basis as necessary. For example selecting the OUTSTANDING ITEMS ONLY will mean that only those items that are still outstanding will be shown.

It is sensible to set up the defaults for the most used data and then you only have to alter some of the individual accounts.

Supplier Defaults

The same comments apply to this as to the Customer Defaults above.

Product Defaults

The screen is slightly different but it works in a similar way to the previous default screens.

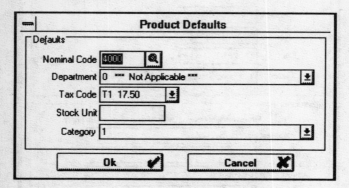

Tax Codes

This displays a dialog box which allows you to alter the active (usable) codes and the VAT rate applicable to them.

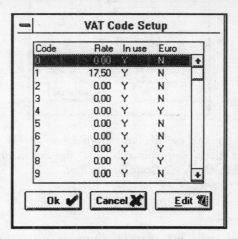

Sage recommend the following codes are used.

T0	zero rated
T1	standard rate
T2	exempt
T4	standard rate sales to EC customers (outside the UK)
T7	zero rate purchases from EC (outside the UK)
T8	standard rate purchases from EC (outside the UK)
T9	non vat transactions

To change any of the codes highlight them and then click on the EDIT button.

The screen will display the next dialog box.

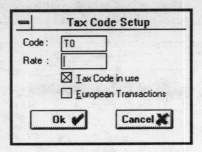

You can enter the details and then click on OK to save it.
You should then see the relevant figures and selections
change within the VAT Code Setup box.

Currency

This can be used for reports, there is no multi currency
processing as such.

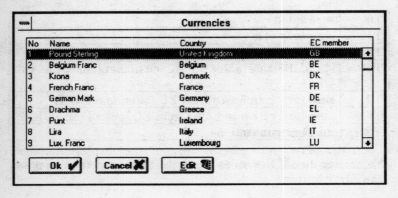

Departments

Here you can setup the departmental structure you want. The dialog box looks like this.

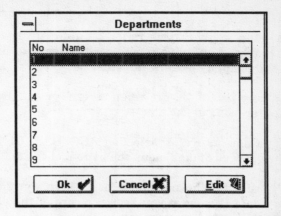

To create departments simply click on the number and then on the EDIT button. Enter the name you want to call the department and then on the OK button and you will see it included in the list.

Product Categories

This works in a very similar way to DEPARTMENTS.

Control Accounts

You can alter the code for any of the displayed control accounts, however I would think very seriously before doing so.

You cannot alter the code for most control accounts once any data has been entered.

Access rights

You can only use this option if you have selected ACCESS RIGHTS within the COMPANY PREFERENCES screen first.

You can setup individual users for the different companies you have created and give them specific rights to different parts of the company ledgers and other data.

This is a very useful feature when several people are using the computer using at the files

To create a new user after selecting ACCESS RIGHTS, you select the NEW command along the bottom of the dialog box.

You will see the following dialog box where you enter the necessary data (I suggest you keep a record of the data you have entered somewhere very secure).

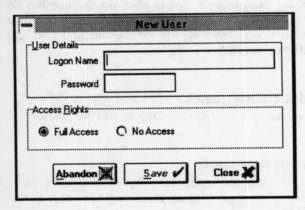

After entering the data the screen will change back to this.

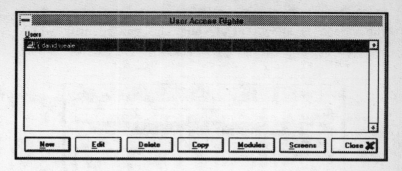

As you can see there are various buttons along the bottom of
the screen and these are explained below.

New
To create a new user.

Edit
To alter a user's details

Delete
To remove a user

Copy
To copy a user's access rights to another user

Modules

The screen is shown below and lets you identify which modules the specific user can access and what rights they have to each.

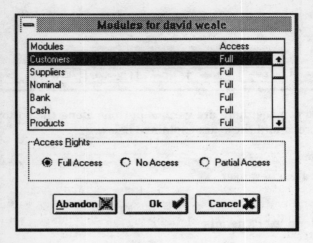

Screens

By double clicking on any named user in the User Access Rights screen you can display all the modules to which they have access.

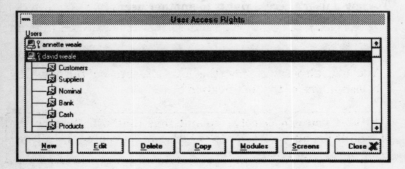

If you then select a specific ledger from the list and click on the SCREENS button, you can allocate rights to the screens within each module.

Report Defaults

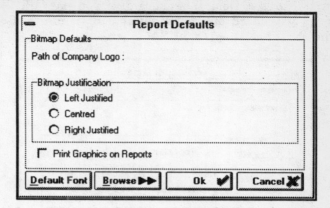

This is rather fun, you can include a company logo or indeed any other (BMP) file within your reports. This could be a logo you have created yourself or an image you have scanned.

To locate the image click on the BROWSE button and then find the image within the directory structure of your hard disc.

Once you have found it you need to click on the PRINT GRAPHICS ON REPORTS box so that it is selected (has an X in it).

You can also select how the logo appears on the page by selecting one of the justification boxes.

In v2.1 you can select a default font that will then be the default for all your reports (which can, of course, be altered for individual reports).

Wallpaper Defaults

As you can see from the dialog box you can BROWSE through your hard disc for a suitable BMP file to use as wallpaper (a backdrop) to the SAGE screen.

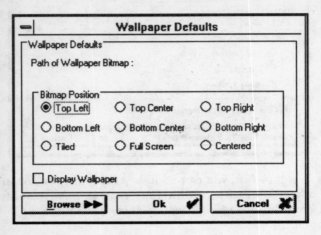

Once you have found a suitable file then you can select to display it in various ways on the screen.

Below you can see a illustration my daughter produced
which has now become (very temporarily) the wallpaper
(shown full screen).

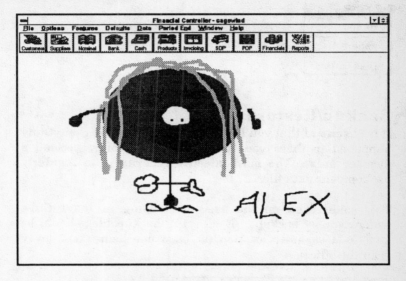

You can either display the wallpaper or not by clicking on
the DISPLAY WALLPAPER box.

Toolbar

The final default that can be set is to hide or display the
TOOLBAR. This will either show the buttons for the
modules or hide them. Obviously if you hide the toolbar
then you will have to use the OPTIONS menu to select the
modules.

Data menu

Here you have four main choices as shown below.

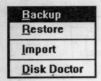

Backup/Restore

It is **essential** that you BACKUP your data files; if anything happened to these your business could rapidly become a disaster area. The most effective security is to regularly backup your data files.

This could work on the basis of keeping **at least** three generations of backups. Each set of backup files should be kept in a separate location (at least one being kept away from the office).

Always **label** the backup discs clearly

The generations may work like this:

❑   A backup is made using a new set of discs

❑   Next day another backup is made

❑   The following day a third backup is made

❑   The fourth day the first backup is re-used

❑   The fifth day the second backup is re-used and so on.

❑   A weekly backup is also made on the same principles as above

So whether you choose to back up daily or weekly (or in between) you are keeping three sets of backups on the go.

Another possibility is to keep a daily backup for a week (five sets) and also a weekly backup for the last four weeks and a monthly backup for the last six months (or whatever permutations you choose).

The RESTORE option lets you replace corrupted files (or to replace horrible mistakes) with the last version of your files that you backed up.

There is a considerable difference between BACKUP and RESTORE; if you confuse them then you could end up with no data files at all.

The BACKUP dialog box (v2.1) looks like this.

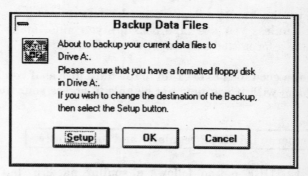

If you select SETUP then the dialog box changes to that shown below. You can then alter the drive or directory to which you want to backup.

V.2 of the program defaults to backing up to the hard disc, you should change this to a floppy or tape. V.2 also has a slightly different dialog box.

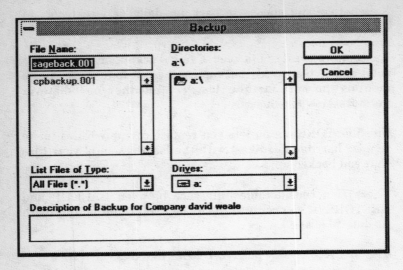

When you backup to a floppy disc (the default and a sensible method unless you use tape backup), you must make sure you have a formatted and empty disc before starting.

It is not a good idea to back up to the hard disc as if you have a problem with it you may not be able to access your files at all !.

Remember to BACKUP regularly and consistently.

The RESTORE option follows a similar pattern, but you must be careful to ensure that the company you wish to restore the data files for is open.

As a safety measure you may like to test your discs before use by using a utility such as NORTON DISK DOCTOR or PCTOOLS DISKFIX so that you can be sure that they will function satisfactorily. I would certainly purchase the best quality discs for use in backing up and replace them at regular intervals.

If you want to know more about directories and their structure any good book on disc operating systems (DOS) will help.

Import

You can import only one type of file format which is the CSV or comma separated file type. You are given the option of choosing the type of transaction the imported data applies to and then you can enter the filename of the imported data file and then RUN the importing.

The dialog box looks like this.

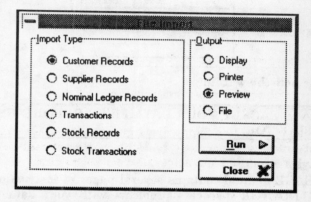

V.2 dialog box is slightly different.

Disk Doctor

This is both a diagnostic feature of the program which will check and correct errors within your SAGE files and allows you to correct certain mistakes.

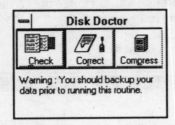

Please note the warning.

ALWAYS BACKUP YOUR DATA FILES **BEFORE** USING DISK DOCTOR.

Check

The SAGE manual contains several pages of instructions if DISK DOCTOR discovers problems with your data files. Unless you are happy to carry out the instructions, I would suggest calling in an expert.

Correct

This part of the DISK DOCTOR helps you alter misposted data. Only some data fields can be changed using this option

When you select the CORRECT option you will be shown the AUDIT TRAIL and you can scroll down this to select the transaction you want to alter.

To do this, highlight the item and then select the EDIT button, make the alteration (if possible) and click on the OK button.

If you alter the transaction date you may also have to alter the payment date.

You can also reverse a transaction using this feature by altering the value to ZERO. This will effectively mean that the transaction never took place. These changes will show up on the AUDIT TRAIL.

> If the VAT has changed then it may be best to carry out a reverse posting i.e. zero the original values and enter the transaction again.

There are various restrictions with this option and a thorough reading of the SAGE program manual would be wise before attempting to alter the data.

> Whenever carrying out these corrections it would be very sensible to print out the AUDIT TRAIL to ensure that the effect of the changes is what you want to happen, remember if in doubt ask your accountant to check.

Compress

You can use it to compress the data files so that empty records are deleted and the file size is reduced.

This is IRREVERSIBLE, so you **must** BACKUP your data files before attempting this.

Period End menu

There are three options here as shown below.

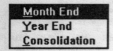

Each deals with separate activities.

Month End

This gives rise to the dialog box shown below.

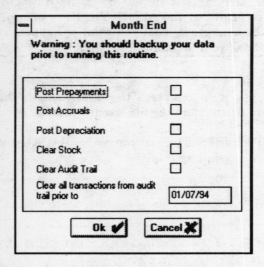

Please note the warning just below the title on the screen.

Warning : You should backup your data prior to running this routine.

Backing up has already been dealt with in an earlier section and is a **VERY IMPORTANT** aspect of any computer system, ignore it at your peril.

The Month End option lets you post the prepayments and accruals that you have set up. These are then entered onto the audit trail.

You can also post the depreciation figures for the month.

Finally you can clear the Audit trail and Stock files for the current month of certain completed transactions.

Year End
The dialog box is shown below.

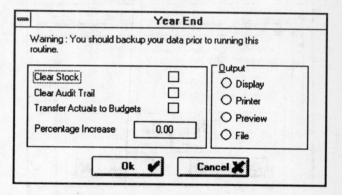

Again there is a warning about backing up the data.

> **Warning : You should backup your data prior to running this routine.**

You can choose to.

Clear Stock
If you select this, you will clear all stock history files.

Clear Audit Trail
Clears certain transactions ready for the new year.

Transfer Actuals to Budgets

This allows you to set the actual figures spent this year as the budget for next, optionally setting a percentage increase for next year's budgets (PERCENTAGE INCREASE).

Consolidation

This lets you consolidate the figures from different companies within your empire to produce consolidated accounts.

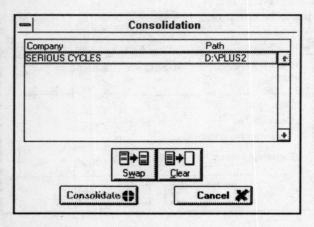

You will be given a list of companies and you select the ones you want to consolidate, the SAGE manual provides a step by step guide for consolidation.

Be careful, the current (displayed) company is (by default) the parent company and all data within it will be deleted. You have been warned.

Window menu

These are standard WINDOWS commands which arrange the (open) windows on the screen.

The one which I find most useful is CLOSE ALL which closes all the open windows returning to the MAIN MENU.

It is worthwhile experimenting with each of the commands if you are unfamiliar with them.

Help menu

This follows the normal WINDOWS conventions. The initial screen is shown below which can be accessed by function key F1 or from the HELP menu (INDEX).

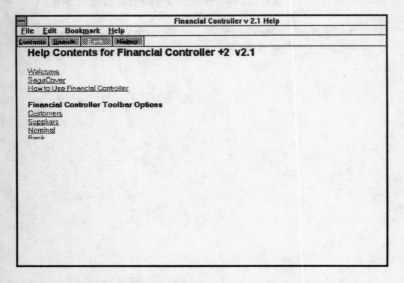

You can use the SEARCH button to display a dialog box. You then type in the topic you are interested in and click on the SHOW TOPICS and then after selecting the relevant topic, click on the GOTO button and a screen will be displayed with the required help.

Note that certain words are coloured green. If you move the cursor onto them a hand will appear.

Those fully underlined mean that there is a further help screen on that topic, those with a dotted line underneath give rise to a text box explaining the word or phrase.

Version 2.1 includes context sensitive help. This means that if you press the **F1** key from anywhere within the program, you will be given help on that section of the program.

The Modules

As you can see from the screen below, the modules are laid
out just below the menu bar. This is called the toolbar.

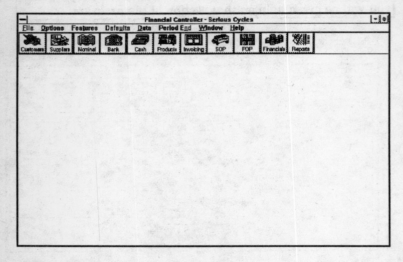

We will look at each of these in turn.

Customers

The CUSTOMERS option is the Sage equivalent of the SALES ledger. The initial screen looks like this.

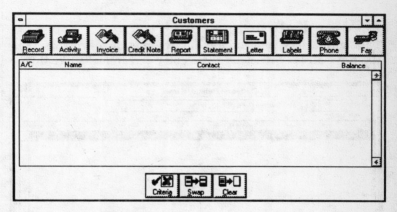

However, before dealing with this, let us look at what is offered by the FEATURES option (available from the pull down menus along the top of the main menu).

Customer Features

There are five options, each is dealt with in sequence.

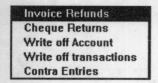

Invoice Refunds

This option lets you account for refunds on payments that you have already received. The entry screen looks like this.

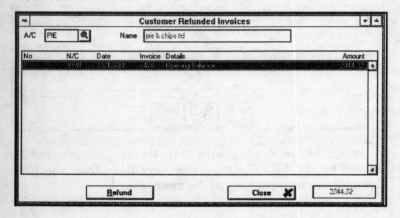

Select the A/C code you want and then highlight the relevant payment and click on the REFUND button. Another screen will appear which is a fail-safe to ensure that you really want to do this and have not made a mistake.

The adjustment will also appear in the bank account.

If you are using VAT CASH ACCOUNTING, Sage advises that you do not use this option.

Cheque Returns

Very similar to the REFUND option, you will be presented with a screen containing the cheques received from the specified customer.

This option lets you cancel a cheque receipt that has bounced.

If you are using VAT CASH ACCOUNTING, Sage advises that you do not use this option.

Write Off Account

You can write off any account by choosing this option. The screen will display the outstanding amounts on the account you have selected.

You should highlight the items you want to write off.

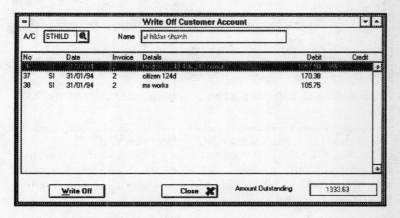

If you select the WRITE OFF button there is a further screen to check you really want to do this.

There is no adjustment for VAT within this option.

Write Off Transactions

You will be asked for the maximum value for any one transaction that you wish to write off. You should then press the TAB key.

The screen will then display all outstanding transactions below this amount and you highlight the ones you want to write off.

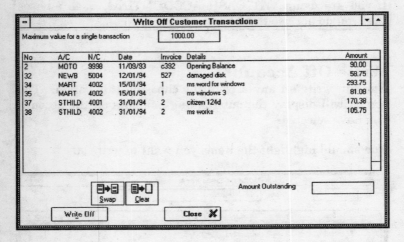

Again there is a further screen to check you really want to do this.

Note that the write off does NOT affect the VAT.

Contra Entries

This option lets you set invoices from customers and suppliers against each other.

For example in the event that a customer is also a supplier you can set invoices of equal values against each other. The screen looks like this.

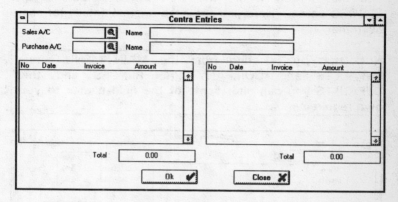

If you use VAT CASH ACCOUNTING there must be identical VAT codes for the items.

Version 2.1 allows partial payments to be offset.

Record

Record

The first button within the CUSTOMER screen is the
RECORD option. Here you enter the original details for each
customer.

Note that by selecting from the MAIN MENU screen
DEFAULTS and COMPANY PREFERENCES and then
DEFAULTS you can alter some of the field names to your
own requirements.

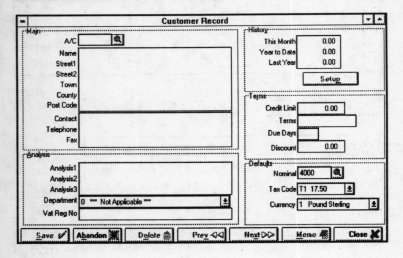

A/C
Each customer must be allocated an A/C code. This code
will be used throughout the program to both call up the
customer details and to analyse the accounts.

Each code must be unique (in fact if you try to use an
already existing code the screen will fill up with the details
you have entered for that code).

Some considerable thought should be given to the allocation of account codes, the more carefully and logically you do this, the more structured and workable your system will be.

It is always worthwhile arranging the structure so that you can easily add new customers when necessary.

Account codes can be up to six characters and made up of any combination of letters and numbers.

Probably a combination of letters and numbers is suitable for most purposes but you need to think about this in the context of your own business.

Name / Street 1 / Street 2 / Town / County / Post Code

These can be up to 30 characters and are used in various parts of the program including stationery and address labels.

Obviously every customer will need to be entered and you may wish to have several records for some customers where you are dealing with different branches or departments of that customer (be careful with the A/C codes).

Contact

The person you normally deal with, again this can be up to 30 characters long and can be printed on address labels.

Telephone / Fax

The actual numbers to be dialled, the phone can be used by the automatic dialler (see the PHONE icon on the right of the main customer screen).

Analysis

These three fields let you analyse the account by whatever criteria you wish (for example by a salesperson's name). This can be used within the reporting structure to produce detailed reports (for example sales per salesperson).

Department

You can allocate the customer to a specific department within your organisation. This can then be used for analysis purposes when you produce reports.

Tax ID

Your customer's Country Code and VAT number.

This Month

This shows the total figure for transactions that have been entered in the current month, it is zeroed when the MONTH END option is carried out.

Year to Date

The total transactions for the year to date, it is zeroed by the running the YEAR END option.

Last Year

This figure automatically results from running the YEAR END option and is the total transaction figure for the previous financial year. You can enter it yourself if you are starting the program for the first time and have therefore do not have a year's figures yet.

Setup

To set up the figures use the SETUP option, you have to save the current record before you can do this.

This lets you enter outstanding invoices. These are added to the DEBTORS CONTROL ACCOUNT and give rise to a SUSPENSE ACCOUNT balance (a similar process takes place when you use the SETUP option within the SUPPLIERS module only this time they are added to the CREDITORS CONTROL ACCOUNT). For more details see Appendix two.

Credit Limit

The amount you want to set for each account. You do not have to set any figure if you do not want to. Entering a figure does not stop you issuing invoices to the customer if the limit is exceeded but it will show up on the AGED analysis (within the ACTIVITY section). An asterisk will be displayed after the account code.

If you enter a credit limit, you will be warned if an invoice exceeds the customer's credit limit.

Terms / Due Days / Discount

The trading terms you use with that customer and the number of days they have to pay from the date of the invoice or any settlement discounts.

Nominal

The sales code for that customer, at present it is set for 4000 but can be altered to any sales code you may wish.

The coding structure is explained within the NOMINAL LEDGER section.

Tax Code

The VAT rate applicable to that customer.

Currency

You can set this to a variety of different currencies, however this is a memorandum for you as SAGE does not carry out multi currency processing.

Memo

You can add any additional text you wish.

Activity

You have three choices, the default displays the Turnover for the year to date, the Credit Limit and the Balance on the account.

You can also select either AGED or HISTORY.

The AGED display will show the amount owing for each account aged over several different periods.

An example screen is shown below.

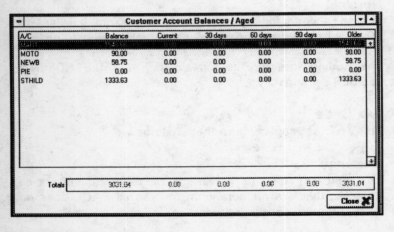

The HISTORY displays the transactions on the accounts and outstanding items are asterisked, a **P** means partly paid.

Again a sample screen is shown below.

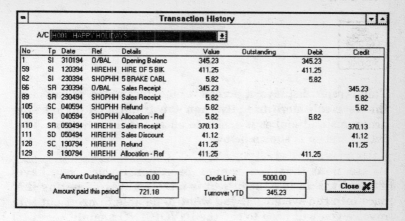

No	Tp	Date	Ref	Details	Value	Outstanding	Debit	Credit
1	SI	310194	O/BAL	Opening Balanc	345.23		345.23	
59	SI	120394	HIREHH	HIRE OF 5 BIK	411.25		411.25	
62	SI	230394	SHOPHH	5 BRAKE CABL	5.82		5.82	
66	SR	230394	O/BAL	Sales Receipt	345.23			345.23
89	SR	290494	SHOPHH	Sales Receipt	5.82			5.82
105	SC	040594	SHOPHH	Refund	5.82			5.82
106	SI	040594	SHOPHH	Allocation - Ref	5.82		5.82	
110	SR	050494	HIREHH	Sales Receipt	370.13			370.13
111	SD	050494	HIREHH	Sales Discount	41.12			41.12
128	SC	190794	HIREHH	Refund	411.25			411.25
129	SI	190794	HIREHH	Allocation - Ref	411.25		411.25	

Amount Outstanding: 0.00

Amount paid this period: 721.18

Credit Limit: 5000.00

Turnover YTD: 345.23

Close

Invoice

This option displays a screen which resembles an invoice, this is much more friendly than the traditional accounting programs and makes it easier to enter the information. The actual screen is shown below.

Please note that you cannot print an invoice you have entered within this module, it is merely a way of getting the data into the system. If you want to be able to print out the invoice you will need to use the INVOICING module.

Using this module does not update the stock records, whereas if you use the INVOICING module you can do so automatically.

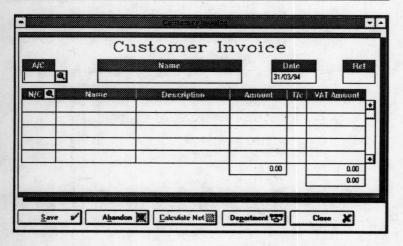

As before you use the TAB key or click with the mouse pointer, to move from field to field within the form.

A/C

The account code for the customer (remember that you can click on the magnifying glass button to display all the existing codes). Once this has been entered then the name of the customer is automatically entered.

Date

By default this is the system date but it can be altered as necessary.

Ref

You can enter a reference for the invoice

N/C and Name

You do the same with the N/C box.

N/C means the Nominal Code and refers to the code for the item being invoiced. The sales codes are within the 4000 series of codes. Entering a code will produce the name of the N/C automatically assuming it already exists.

You can create a new code by selecting NEW from the dialog box that appears.

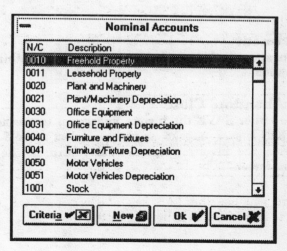

Description
You then enter the description of the item.

Amount
Enter the amount and the VAT will be calculated (remember to check the VAT rate is correct for that item). The total column will be calculated and the cumulative total also.

Adding items to the invoice
Simply TAB onto the next line of the form and continue as before. You are not limited to the number of items shown initially as you can carry on below. As you enter more items, the cumulative total will alter.

The Buttons
The are several buttons along the bottom of the window, these are described below.

Calculate Net
Very useful, if you have entered the gross amount, you can click on this button and the VAT will be calculated on the amount and then the program will **deduct** the VAT. This could be used if you are only given the amount inclusive of VAT.

Department
You can allocate this invoice to a department within your organisation.

Save, Abandon, Close
You can either SAVE the invoice and go on to the next, or ABANDON it as a mistake, or you can select CLOSE which exits from the invoicing option and return to the main customer screen.

Credit Note

This is the opposite of the Invoice option and the entries are made in the same way.

It is important to make sure the codes you use are the same as the original for matching purposes.

Report

Report

The initial screen lets you choose from several different reports, four of which are already set up for you. These are reports on Activity (a history of customer transactions), Balances (Balance, Turnover, Aged Debts, etc.), Customer List and VAT List.

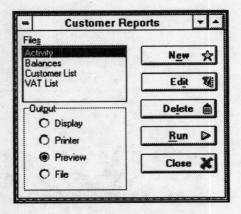

The buttons on the right of the dialog box are described below.

New

This produces the following screen.

```
┌─────────────────────────────────────────────────────┐
│ ▬│        Customer Report Creation                    │
│ ┌─────────────────────────────────────────────────┐ │
│ │ ☐ A/C          ☐ Fax          ☐ Terms           │ │
│ │ ☐ Name         ☐ Analysis1    ☐ Due Days        │ │
│ │ ☐ Full Address ☐ Analysis2    ☐ Tax Code        │ │
│ │ ☐ Street1      ☐ Analysis3    ☐ Balance (Current)│ │
│ │ ☐ Street2      ☐ Balance      ☐ 30 - 60 Days    │ │
│ │ ☐ Town         ☐ Credit Limit ☐ 60 - 90 Days    │ │
│ │ ☐ County       ☐ This Month   ☐ 90 - 120 Days   │ │
│ │ ☐ Post Code    ☐ YTD          ☐ Balance (Older) │ │
│ │ ☐ Contact      ☐ Last Year                       │ │
│ │ ☐ Telephone                   Report width  ▭   │ │
│ ├─────────────────────────────────────────────────┤ │
│ │ ┌──────────────────┐     ┌──────────────────┐   │ │
│ │ │   Save      ✔    │     │   Cancel    ✖   │   │ │
│ │ └──────────────────┘     └──────────────────┘   │ │
│ └─────────────────────────────────────────────────┘ │
└─────────────────────────────────────────────────────┘
```

You click on the fields you want to include in the report and then SAVE the form. You will be prompted for a filename which you can decide upon.

Once you have saved this file the name you give it will appear with the other reports.

Edit

This option loads whatever report file you have highlighted from the list. You can then alter the file and save it in its new version.

You cannot edit the fixed (original) reports.

Delete

You can delete any of the files you have created by highlighting them and then choosing this option. There is a further dialog box which asks if you are sure.

You cannot delete the fixed (original) reports.

Run

This will merge the chosen report with the highlighted customers in the box displaying the customers. If no customers are highlighted then all will be included in the report.

Close

Click on this when you have finished with the option and the screen will return to the previous menu.

Output

You can display the report on the screen (DISPLAY) or send it to the PRINTER or to a FILE for future use, you can also PREVIEW it so that you can alter the fonts, etc., before printing out (see Appendix five for an explanation of PREVIEW).

Statement

This generates a statement for the selected customers. You can alter the time period by changing the start/end date and you can choose a different file by using the BROWSE option.

Letter

Selecting this option will bring up the following screen.

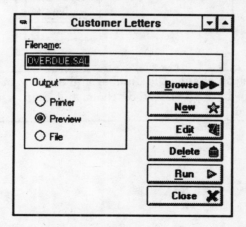

You can generate a letter requesting payment of an overdue amount or you create your own letters.

Labels

Labels

You can print labels to your customers by selecting this option. You can preview the labels, send them to a printer or to a file for future use.

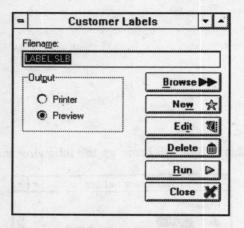

In v2.1 you can change the number and position of the labels on the page by PREVIEWING them and then selecting the LAYOUT button.

Phone / Fax

Assuming that your computer is connected to the Phone via a modem or to a fax machine (or has an internal fax card) then these options let you communicate with the outside world via the program.

Please note that the FAX option produces a document suitable for sending via a fax, it does not actually send the fax.

Suppliers

Effectively a mirror image of the CUSTOMERS option. This is the PURCHASE ledger as it is called in traditional accounting systems.

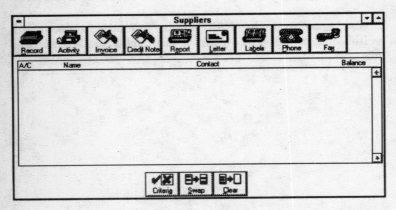

As you can see from the icons shown above the options within the SUPPLIERS menu are very similar to those within the CUSTOMERS. The only one missing is the STATEMENT which is obviously not needed.

The FEATURES available along the top of the screen are also very similar. The only real difference between them is the absence from the FEATURES menu of the option of CONTRA ENTRIES.

Nominal

Nominal

The Nominal Ledger, the opening screen looks like this.

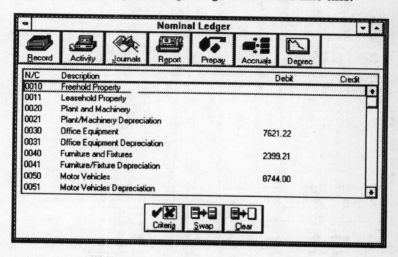

This shows a list of the Nominal Accounts with the debit or credit balance on each.

Below is a list of the account codes available.

Code	Description
0010	Freehold Property
0011	Leasehold Property
0020	Plant and Machinery
0021	Plant/Machinery Depreciation
0030	Office Equipment
0031	Office Equipment Depreciation
0040	Furniture and Fixtures
0041	Furniture/Fixture Depreciation
0050	Motor Vehicles
0051	Motor Vehicles Depreciation
1001	Stock
1002	Work in Progress
1003	Finished Goods
1100	Debtors Control Account
1101	Sundry Debtors
1102	Other Debtors
1103	Prepayments
1200	Bank Current Account
1210	Bank Deposit Account
1220	Building Society Account
1230	Petty Cash
2100	Creditors Control Account
2101	Sundry Creditors
2102	Other Creditors
2109	Accruals
2200	Sales Tax Control Account
2201	Purchase Tax Control Account
2202	VAT Liability
2210	P.A.Y.E.
2211	National Insurance
2230	Pension Fund
2300	Loans
2310	Hire Purchase
2320	Corporation Tax
2330	Mortgages
3000	Ordinary Shares
3001	Preference Shares
3100	Reserves
3101	Undistributed Reserves
3200	Profit and Loss Account
3333	
4000	Sales Type A
4001	Sales Type B
4002	Sales Type C
4009	Discounts Allowed
4100	Sales Type D
4101	Sales Type E
4200	Sales of Assets
4900	Miscellaneous Income
4901	Royalties Received
4902	Commissions Received
4903	Insurance Claims
4904	Rent Income
4905	Distribution and Carriage
5000	Materials Purchases
5001	Materials Imported
5002	Miscellaneous Purchases
5003	Packaging
5009	Discounts Taken
5100	Carriage
5101	Import Duty
5102	Transport Insurance
5200	Opening Stock
5201	Closing Stock
6000	Productive Labour
6001	Cost of Sales Labour
6002	Sub-Contractors
6100	Sales Commissions
6200	Sales Promotions
6201	Advertising
6202	Gifts and Samples
6203	P.R. (Literature & Brochures)
6900	Miscellaneous Expenses
7001	Directors Salaries
7002	Directors Remuneration
7003	Staff Salaries
7004	Wages - Regular
7005	Wages - Casual
7006	Employers N.I.
7007	Employers Pensions
7008	Recruitment Expenses
7100	Rent
7102	Water Rates
7103	General Rates
7104	Premises Insurance
7200	Electricity
7201	Gas
7202	Oil
7203	Other Heating Costs
7300	Fuel and Oil
7301	Repairs and Servicing
7302	Licences
7303	Vehicle Insurance
7304	Miscellaneous Motor Expenses
7400	Travelling
7401	Car Hire
7402	Hotels
7403	U.K. Entertainment
7404	Overseas Entertainment
7405	Overseas Travelling
7406	Subsistence
7500	Printing
7501	Postage and Carriage
7502	Telephone
7503	Telex/Telegram/Facsimile
7504	Office Stationery
7505	Books etc.
7600	Legal Fees
7601	Audit and Accountancy Fees
7602	Consultancy Fees
7603	Professional Fees
7700	Equipment Hire
7701	Office Machine Maintenance
7800	Repairs and Renewals
7801	Cleaning
7802	Laundry
7803	Premises Expenses
7900	Bank Interest Paid
7901	Bank Charges
7902	Currency Charges
7903	Loan Interest Paid
7904	H.P. Interest
7905	Credit Charges
8000	Depreciation
8001	Plant/Machinery Depreciation
8002	Furniture/Fitting Depreciation
8003	Vehicle Depreciation
8004	Office Equipment Depreciation
8100	Bad Debt Write Off
8102	Bad Debt Provision
8200	Donations
8201	Subscriptions
8202	Clothing Costs
8203	Training Costs
8204	Insurance
8205	Refreshments
9998	Suspense Account
9999	Mispostings Account

Code Groupings

The groups of codes for the accounts are shown below, they can of course be altered to suit your organisational needs.

To alter them simply click on the FINANCIALS button and then select LAYOUT and then choose to EDIT and change the descriptions and number range for any of the account headings. Remember to SAVE the changes.

```
Profit & Loss

    Sales

    Product Sales            4000    to    4099
    Export Sales             4100    to    4199
    Sales of Assets          4200    to    4299
    Other Sales              4900    to    4999

    Purchases

    Purchases                5000    to    5099
    Purchase Charges         5100    to    5199
    Stock                    5200    to    5299

    Direct Expenses

    Labour                   6000    to    6099
    Commissions              6100    to    6199
    Sales Promotion          6200    to    6299
    Miscellaneous Expenses   6900    to    6999

    Overheads

    Salaries and Wages       7000    to    7099
    Rent and Rates           7100    to    7199
    Heat, Light and Power    7200    to    7299
    Motor Expenses           7300    to    7399
    Travelling and Ent.      7400    to    7499
    Printing and Stationery  7500    to    7599
    Professional Fees        7600    to    7699
    Equipment Hire & Rent    7700    to    7799
    Maintenance              7800    to    7899
    Bank Charges & Interest  7900    to    7999
    Depreciation             8000    to    8099
    Bad Debts                8100    to    8199
    General Expenses         8200    to    8299
```

Balance Sheet

Fixed Assets

Property	0010	to	0019
Plant and Machinery	0020	to	0029
Office Equipment	0030	to	0039
Furniture and Fixtures	0040	to	0049
Motor Vehicles	0050	to	0059

Current Assets

Stock	1000	to	1099
Debtors	1100	to	1199
Deposits and Cash	1210	to	1299
Bank Account	1200	to	1209
VAT Liability	2200	to	2209

Current Liabilities

Creditors : Short Term	2100	to	2199
Taxation	2210	to	2299
Creditors : Long Term	2300	to	2399
Bank Account	1200	to	1209
VAT Liability	2200	to	2209

Financed By

Share Capital	3000	to	3099
Reserves	3100	to	3299

Note how the BANK A/C and VAT LIABILITY are shown as both CURRENT ASSETS and CURRENT LIABILITIES. This is simply because they can be assets or liabilities depending upon whether you are owed money or owe it.

Record

Record

You can identify a nominal account from the list by clicking on it, you can then record or alter certain data about that account (e.g. the name you want to call the account) by selecting the RECORD button.

You can also set up totally new account codes that did not previously exist. This is useful as you may have several more types of purchases (for example) than the program has set up for you. To do this enter a new code in the N/C box after selecting the RECORD button.

When adding new codes make sure that they are within the correct groups for the type of transactions you will be dealing with.

Notes: The opening balance for Nominal Accounts can be SETUP **or** can be entered by JOURNAL. The AUDIT TRAIL will show a JD (journal debit) or JC (journal credit) whichever method is used.

If you use SETUP to enter the opening balances please print the TRIAL BALANCE when you have finished to make sure that you have made no errors and do not have any SUSPENSE balances.

An empty record data screen is shown below.

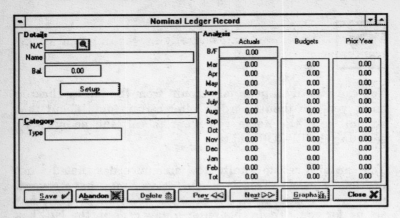

Some of the fields are self explanatory, the others are:

Setup
To set up the details when starting SAGE for the first time
(i.e. the figures that exist prior to setting it up).

The Setup screen looks like this.

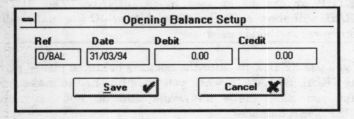

As you can see you are able to enter a debit or credit balance.

Note the date is always shown as the system date and you
may need to alter this.

The Analysis

Actuals
These will be entered automatically by the program as the months go on.

Budget
You enter the budget figures if you want to. The beauty of doing this is that the actual and budgeted figures can be compared with each other so that you can easily see any discrepancies and act upon the information.

Prior Year
You can enter the previous year's figures.

Graphs
You can produce graphs of the figures.

A useful option shown along the bottom of the screen of the graph screen lets you COPY the chart so that you can include it any WINDOWS application for instance within a word processed report.

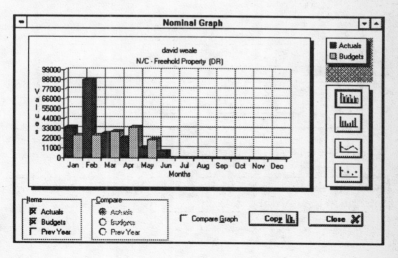

In v2.1 you can choose 3D or 2D bar charts as well as line graphs or scatter charts. In the Nominal record Graph you can also compare two sets of data by selecting the COMPARE GRAPH box.

Activity

This, like previous modules, lets you display a history of any selected accounts. If you do not select an account all will be displayed in sequence.

Journals

Journals

A journal is used to make adjustments to the data you have
entered, e.g. mispostings or to make specific entries, e.g.
adjustment to the closing stock.

This is where a knowledge of double entry techniques can be
useful.

The data entry screen looks like this.

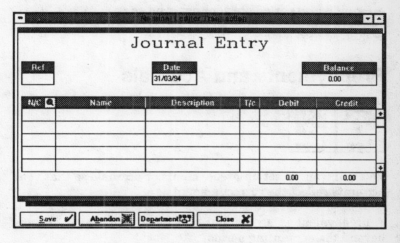

You enter the data in the appropriate field.

Note you cannot finish or SAVE a journal unless the
cumulative total for the debit column is the same as the
cumulative total for the credit column i.e. the balance is zero.

The buttons include one for DEPARTMENT so that you can
allocate a journal to a specific department within your
organisation.

Note that the date for the JOURNAL entry (as for all entries into SAGE) is very important as SAGE groups data according to the date of the transaction.

Report

The reporting option follows the same method as the one within the CUSTOMERS option, you can display or edit the existing reports or create your own and so on.

Prepayments and Accruals

You will want to set up prepayments or accruals so that your accounts reflect the correct amounts.

A prepayment is an amount you have paid which extends beyond the accounting period.

An accrual is (e.g.) when you owe money for an expense that has not been invoiced to you.

To do this you select PREPAYMENTS (or ACCRUALS) and you will see the following data entry screen (headed either PREPAYMENTS or ACCRUALS).

Prepayments

N/C 🔍	Description	Value	Mth	Net Amount	Pst

[Save ✔]   [Cancel ✖]

The data that is not self-explanatory is:

Mth
The number of months the amount is to be spread over.

Value
The amount of the Prepayment or Accrual (net of VAT).

Net Amount
The amount of the prepayment or accrual. This is calculated automatically.

Pst
The number of months that the accrual / prepayment has been posted to the accounts. This is entered automatically by the program and is the result of running the MONTH END routine.

When you have entered the data then you click on the SAVE button.

Deleting prepayments or accruals
Move the cursor or click in the relevant row and press the function key F6.

Depreciation

Deprec

This is the reduction in value of an asset due to time or wear and tear. By selecting this you will get the entry screen shown below.

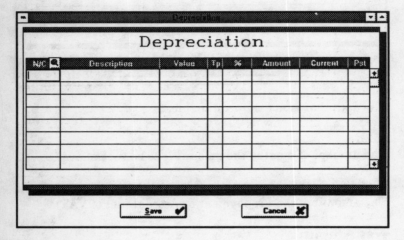

The data fields that need explanation are:

Value
The value of the asset, normally its cost, however if you are setting up SAGE from existing records and/or are using the REDUCING BALANCE method then the net book value of the asset.

Tp
The type of depreciation you are using. There are three methods available to you.

Straight Line (S)
The same amount is deducted from the cost of the asset every period.

Thus if an asset cost £1000 and you decided to depreciate it at 10% per annum, the depreciation would be £100 per annum until the value was reduced to zero.

This can be seen clearly from the following table.

Year	Net Book Value	Depreciation
One	1000	100
Two	900	100
Three	800	100
Four	700	100

Reducing Balance (R)
This is slightly different. Here the depreciation for each period is deducted from the initial figure and then the next period's depreciation is calculated on the **reduced balance**.

Year	Net Book Value	Depreciation
One	1000	100
Two	900	90
Three	810	81
Four	729	73

Write Off (W)
The total amount is written off in the period. Normally this will be used to write off small amounts outstanding when the reduced balance method is used or where the asset becomes suddenly worthless.

%
The percentage you want to depreciate the asset per annum.

Amount
Once the preceding data has been entered this will be calculated automatically. Note that the depreciation per month is the yearly figure (not shown) divided by twelve.

Current
The current value.

Pst
The number of times the asset has been depreciated.

When finished you can SAVE the data.

Deleting an item
Move the cursor to the line and then press the function key
F6, be very careful as there is no fail-safe, if you accidentally
delete an item it may be better to cancel the screen rather
than save it.

Bank

Bank

This deals with the bank accounts of your business. After selecting this the following screen will be displayed.

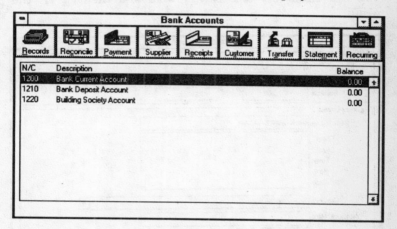

As you can see there is a list of the bank account codes, this includes the defaults and any you create by using the RECORD option (see below) together with the balance on each of the accounts.

Records

This will let you set up new bank accounts.

You can enter any details you wish and then SAVE the result.

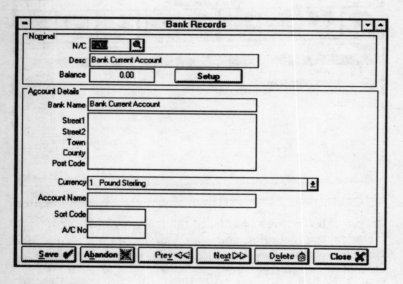

Sort Code
This is entered as NN-NN-NN.

Reconcile

Reconcile

After selecting this the screen shown below will be displayed.

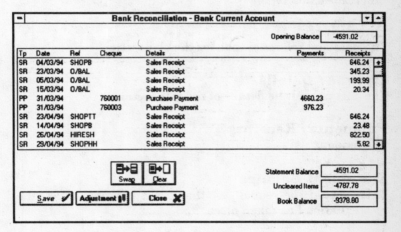

All transactions that have been entered into the computer will be shown for the chosen bank account (only one bank account can be shown at any one time).

The idea is that you reconcile or agree the transactions on your real bank account with those in your computer, by adding additional transactions to adjust for bank charges, interest and any other items that have not been entered into the computer.

The various fields are:

Opening Balance
This is the brought forward figure from the previous reconciliation.

Tp
The transaction type.

Date / Ref
The date and reference code for the transaction.

Cheque / Details
The cheque and the details of the transaction.

Payments / Receipts
The amount.

Statement Balance
This should be equal to the book balance after the reconciliation has taken place.

Uncleared Items
A total of the unreconciled amounts that appear on the screen.

Book Balance
The difference between the statement balance and the uncleared items.

How to reconcile

❑ Click on the RECONCILE button, this will display all the recorded transactions in the chosen bank account that have not been previously reconciled.

❑ Note that as you highlight items the STATEMENT and UNCLEARED ITEMS balances change.

❑ Highlight all those items that agree with the bank account statement.

❑ Click on the ADJUSTMENT button to add items that are on the bank statement but not on the computer.

❑ Make sure the BALANCES on the screen now are equal to the bank balance on your statement and save the reconciliation. (Unless, of course, there are items showing on the screen that have not been cleared through the bank in which case they will be included in the total uncleared items box).

Note that any ADJUSTMENTS are written to the NOMINAL LEDGER and will not be reversed even if you abandon the reconciliation before finishing it.

Payment

Payment

This is used for payments where the transaction has not been entered in the supplier ledger.

The data entry screen is shown below.

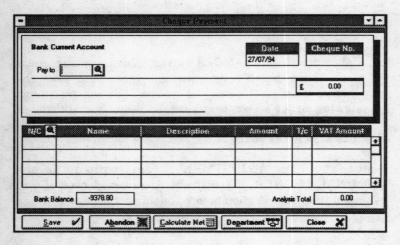

The data entry fields are:

Pay to
By clicking on the button to the right of the box, a list of the suppliers you have accounts for will appear. Select the one you want or leave it blank or create a new supplier account.

Date / Cheque No.
Whatever details you need to enter.

N/C / Name
Select a NOMINAL code for the payment and the Name field will be automatically entered.

Description
Enter a description to identify the transaction.

Amount / T/C / VAT Amount
Enter the amount and either accept the default VAT code
(T1) or change it and the VAT amount will be calculated for
you.

Note how the remaining data is entered for you by the
program, the Bank Balance at the bottom of the screen is
reduced and the amount is entered onto the cheque at the
top.

Adding items
You can continue to add items to the payment by moving
onto the next data entry row below the one you have filled in
and again you will see the other figures automatically
increment without you having to do anything else.

It is very useful to be able to see your bank balance at the
bottom especially when it becomes a negative figure!

When finished you can SAVE or ABANDON the whole
cheque payment. When you have finally finished you can
click on CLOSE to close the window.

There are two other useful buttons along the bottom of the
screen:

Calculate Net
If you enter the AMOUNT and then click on this button, the
VAT is deducted from the payment and entered in the VAT
Amount.

This is different from the normal method where the VAT is
effectively added to the AMOUNT entered.

Department
You can allocate any payment to a specific department by
clicking this button and then selecting the department.

Supplier

Supplier

The screen looks like this.

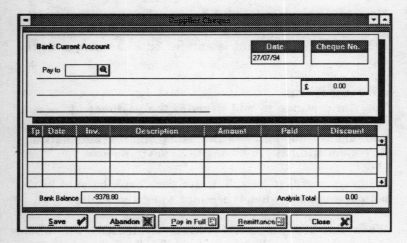

The data entry fields are:

Pay to
By clicking on the button to the right of the box, a list of the
suppliers you have accounts for will appear. Select the one
you want, the screen will fill up with the outstanding
invoices.

When you select the PAID column, the program defaults to
the first in the sequence, if you do not want to pay that one
simply move the cursor onto the next (using the cursor keys).

Date / Cheque No.
Whatever details you need to enter.

Tp / Date / Inv. / Description / Amount

These are all entered automatically by the program and display the unpaid or uncleared transactions on that specific supplier's account.

Discount

If you enter the discount in that field then the value in the paid field will alter to take account of this.

The buttons are similar to the PAYMENTS screen except for two, these are:

Pay In Full

If you click on this when in the PAID field the specific item will be cleared and the payment added to the total.

Remittance

If you want to print a remittance advice (**before** you have saved the data) you can do so by clicking on this button.

Receipt

Receipt

Again this is for use where the item has not been entered into the customer's ledger. The screen for this option is shown below.

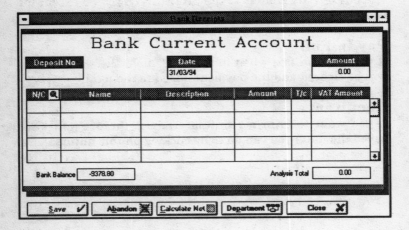

The data to be entered is as follows:

Deposit No.
Here you can enter the cheque number or other details concerning the receipt.

N/C / Name
Select a nominal code and the name (of it) will be automatically entered.

Description
Text which describes the transaction.

Amount / T/C / VAT

You enter the amount, alter the tax code if necessary and the VAT will be calculated automatically.

The buttons are similar to previous options, remember that the CALCULATE NET button enables you to work out the VAT on a gross amount.

Credit card receipts

Nowadays many businesses accept credit cards for sales and you may like to consider the following techniques for dealing with them.

Have separate bank account codes for each credit card company you deal with.

Either post the receipts through the RECEIPTS option or if you want to record the invoice then you will need to enter those details through the CUSTOMER or INVOICING options.

You can transfer the amounts from these special bank accounts to your main account by using the TRANSFER option or by JOURNALISING the amounts.

Any charges made by the credit card company can be adjusted for when you carry out the BANK RECONCILIATION. It is worthwhile using a NOMINAL ACCOUNT CODE for these charges and code 7906 can be set up as being for CREDIT CARD CHARGES (as suggested by SAGE).

Customer

Once you have selected the customer from whom you have received money a list of the amounts outstanding will be displayed.

The data to be entered is similar to previous screens, some of it is entered by the program.

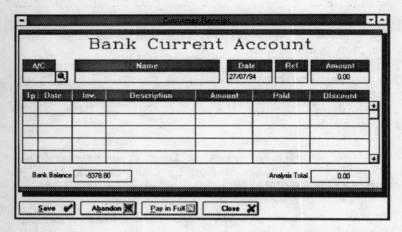

When you select the PAID column, the program defaults to the first in the sequence, if you do not want to pay that one simply move the cursor onto the next (using the cursor keys).

Enter the amount you to pay from the invoice or click on the PAY IN FULL button.

Enter as many items as you want to and then SAVE the data.

Transfer

This enables you to transfer money from one bank account to another.

> Note: To transfer funds from a BANK ACCOUNT to CASH has to be accounted for by using a JOURNAL entry. Be careful to use tax code T9 for this.

Statement

You can preview, print or send the bank statement to a file for future use.

Recurring

This lets you deal with recurring entries, the data entry
screen is shown below.

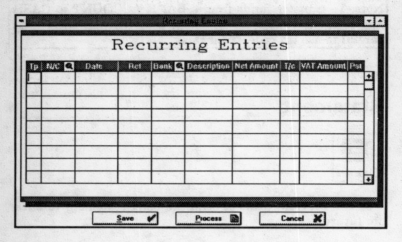

The idea is that you let SAGE deal with entries that occur on
a regular basis. The fields are as follows:

Tp
You have a choice of four entries.

BP / BR	Bank payment or bank receipt
JD / JC	Journal debit or journal credit

N/C / Date / Ref
Enter the relevant data into each of these.

Bank
The bank account you want the entry to be entered into.

Description
A text description.

Net Amount / T/C / VAT Amount
Enter the NET AMOUNT, alter the TAX CODE if necessary and the AMOUNT will be calculated for you.

Pst
A Y entry here shows that the entry has been processed. This is automatically entered by the program.

When the data has been entered, you can save it and PROCESS it.

If you do not process the recurring entries then an error message will appear when you try to run the month end option.

Cash

This option lets you record your cash transactions. The opening screen looks like this.

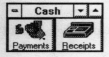

Payments and Receipts

These are dealt with together as the data entry screens are very similar.

The PAYMENTS screen is shown below.

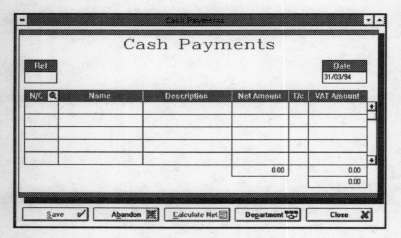

The data entry fields have been dealt with in previous sections as have the buttons along the bottom of the screen.

Note that to transfer funds from a BANK ACCOUNT to CASH has to be accounted for by using a JOURNAL entry. Be careful to use tax code T9 for this.

Products

This is the STOCK CONTROL option within the program, it operates on a FIFO (first in, first out) basis.

The first screen looks like this.

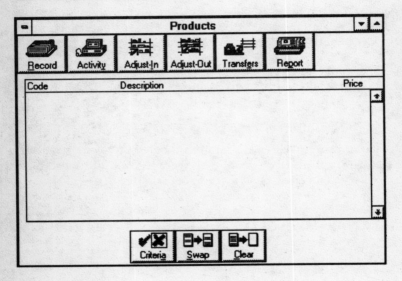

Record

Record

Entering stock details is actually two operations.

The RECORD into which details of the stock item are entered.

Then after this has been done, the actual number of items received or dispatched and their cost is entered using the options ADJUST-IN and ADJUST-OUT.

You have to use the RECORD option to start the process of entering stock, it can also be used to make any amendments or to delete unwanted items.

Warning

It is vitally important to think how you want your stock organised and to spend time working out the most logical and usable system before starting to enter the stock.

Pay particular attention to the codes you use. Remember that you may well introduce or buy new stock items as you expand.

The screen for the recording of the stock details is shown below.

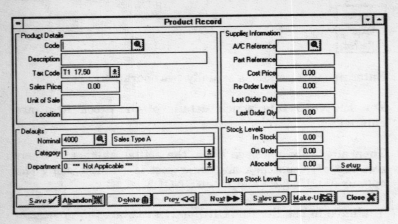

Code
This is the code you wish to assign to that particular stock item. It must be unique and can be up to 16 characters long. You can use F4 or click on the symbol to the right of the field (the FINDER symbol shown below).

Description
A description of the product, up to 30 characters can be used.

Tax Code
The VAT code; normally **T1** which represents the normal VAT rate or one of the other VAT codes if the item is not subject to VAT at the standard rate. Clicking on the arrow to the right of the box will bring up a list of the codes you have set up.

Sales Price
This is the selling price per unit of the product, i.e. the current price **net** of VAT.

Unit of Sale
How many of the item are sold together e.g. a pair.

Location
Where the stock item is stored e.g. a bin or building.

Nominal
The nominal code allocated to this product, this is normally one of the Sales codes (the 4000 series). This code will be used for analysis purposes.

Category
You can organise your stock into different categories e.g. bicycles, tyres, sundries, etc. Remember that these can be set up or altered by using the DEFAULTS menu (along the top of the screen) and then selecting PRODUCT CATEGORIES.

Department
The department that the item will be allocated to, this will be used for analysis purposes.

Supplier Information
Select a supplier and enter any relevant details.

Stock Levels
These show the current stock position if you call up the record at some time after creating it.

The SETUP button can be used to enter the stock holding when you initially create your stock control records. The SETUP button can only be used when you first enter the stock details and you must save the record before you can enter the opening stock details.

If you select IGNORE STOCK LEVELS, the program cannot update stock levels and indeed will not let you add stock by way of ADJUSTMENT IN. It is only to be used for non stock items such as fixed price charges, etc.

The Buttons

Along the bottom of the dialog box are various new buttons. Only certain of them are available depending upon the action you are taking.

Sales

Clicking on this bring up a display of data about the stock item.

Graphs can be produced from this data in a similar way to those in the NOMINAL RECORD option.

Makeup

This lets you enter the make-up of a particular stock item in terms of the components that are needed to make it. For example if you were making a bicycle, it would be made up of wheels, tyres, saddle, chain, sprockets and so on.

Each component must be set up as a stock record before it can be included in the Makeup of another stock item.

The screen is shown below.

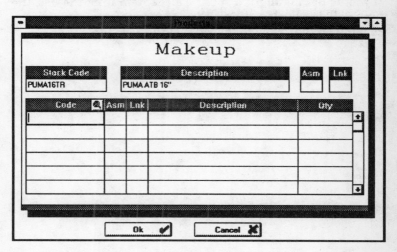

When you have finished entering the stock records and the initial balances, I suggest that you print out a stock valuation (REPORTS and then scroll down the list and select VALUATION). Compare this with the original stock list you entered to ensure that the two match both in total value and in detail.

Activity

This displays the transactions that have taken place within the selected stock items.

If you do not highlight a specific stock item from the list, the first will be displayed and then you can select another by clicking on the arrow to the right of the code box.

Adjustments In / Adjustments Out

This is where the number of items received or issued can be entered. The screens looks like this (this is actually Adjustments In)

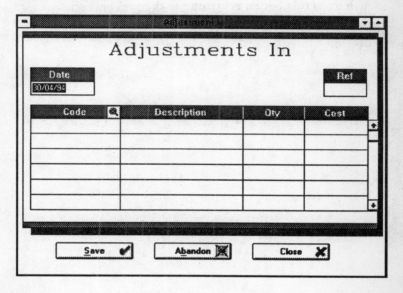

Date
The default is the system date, you can overwrite this with any date you wish.

Ref
If you want to enter a useful reference e.g. a goods received note (GRN).

Code
You can display a list of the current codes by clicking on the button (to the right).

Description / Qty / Cost

Enter the relevant data (there is no column for COST within ADJUSTMENT OUT).

You can enter several items on the same screen, the cursor will move onto the next line automatically.

The buttons along the bottom of the dialog box let you SAVE, ABANDON (the data entry you are currently on) or CLOSE (which exits this option returning to the previous screen).

Note that the COST of the item is updated by the new price used in the posting.

Transfers

Transfers

This is used to transfer components. It can be used to transfer stock items when they are used to make up another stock item.

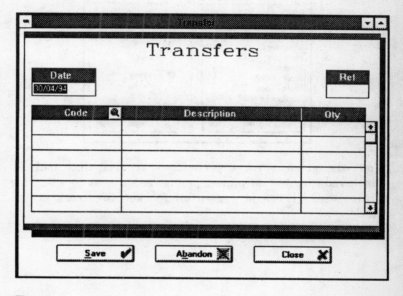

Date
Accept or change the default.

Ref
Any useful data, e.g. the transfer note.

Code
The code of the item to which the stock is being transferred.

Description / Quantity
Enter the relevant data.

Report

As with previous Report options a dialog box is displayed.

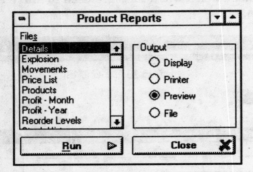

You are given several predefined reports that can be displayed, printed on paper, previewed or sent to a file for future use. These are essential for keeping track of the stock.

Invoicing

Invoicing

Features

Along the top of the MAIN MENU screen you can see the word FEATURES. This has been covered with respect to CUSTOMERS and SUPPLIERS. There is a further option, that of INVOICE FEATURES.

If you select this you will be given a further choice of two options.

Memorise

SAGE can be asked to memorise the invoice which can then be recalled at some future time. This is useful either as a model or for invoices that are regularly sent.

A dialog box will appear into which you enter a name and description for your invoice and then SAVE it.

Recall

Use this to recall a memorised invoice. It will be given the next invoice in sequence and the current (system) date.

Invoicing

The opening screen is shown below.

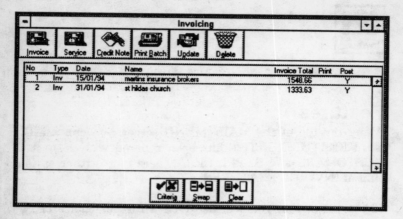

The buttons along the top of the window offer you the opportunity to produce invoices and to update the relevant ledgers.

> Note that you have to use the INVOICING module if you want to print the invoices or automatically update the ledgers and stock records.

Invoice

Invoice

Within this you can produce invoices for customers from your stock records. Your stock records will automatically be reduced (after you have used the UPDATE option).

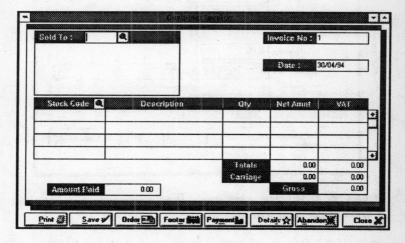

You can enter a NON-STOCK item by using any of the following codes in the STOCK CODE field.

If you enter any of these an additional dialog box (shown below) will appear into which you can enter details of the non stock item.

S1	Taxable non stock item
S2	Zero rated non stock item
M	Text only

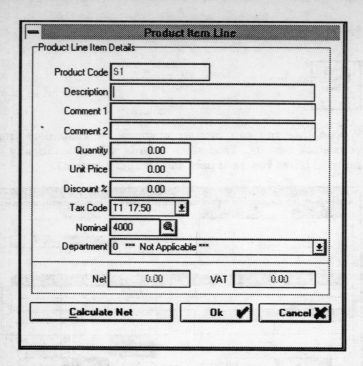

Product Item Line

Product Line Item Details

Product Code `S1`

Description

Comment 1

Comment 2

Quantity `0.00`

Unit Price `0.00`

Discount % `0.00`

Tax Code `T1 17.50`

Nominal `4000`

Department `0 *** Not Applicable ***`

Net `0.00`   VAT `0.00`

[Calculate Net]   [Ok ✔]   [Cancel ✘]

If you try to invoice more items than you actually have then a warning screen will appear.

The VAT is automatically calculated and the totals for the invoice are added up for you.

You can keep adding items to the invoice if you wish.

The buttons along the bottom of the data entry screen are different from those previously met and are explained below.

Print
This will print the invoice.

Save

This will save the details and clear the screen ready for the next invoice. After choosing CLOSE the original screen will appear with details of the saved invoices.

You can edit (change) them by highlighting them and then selecting the INVOICE button or delete them by using the DELETE button if you so wish.

Order

This lets you change the address for the goods and invoices from that of the original which you set up when you created the customer record.

You will see the following screen into which you enter the details.

```
━|                    Order Details
┌─ Order Details ──────────────────────────────────┐
│           Order No.  │  │                          │
│   Customer Order No.  │  │                          │
│  Customer Phone No.  │                          │   │
│          Deliver To  │                          │   │
│           Address 1  │                          │   │
│           Address 2  │                          │   │
│           Address 3  │                          │   │
│           Address 4  │                          │   │
│             Notes 1  │                          │   │
│             Notes 2  │                          │   │
│             Notes 3  │                          │   │
│                          [ Ok  ✔ ]  [ Cancel ✘ ]  │
└──────────────────────────────────────────────────┘
```

Footer

This lets you add certain additional charges to the invoice, any additional carriage and any settlement terms you want to add (as shown below).

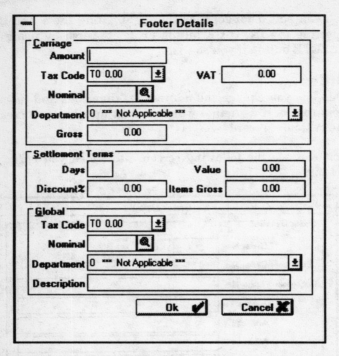

The GLOBAL section enables you to code the whole invoice to a specific TAX or NOMINAL code and DEPARTMENT if you so wish.

Payment

If the customer has made any payments in advance towards this invoice then this can be recorded by selecting the PAYMENT button. The data entry screen is shown below.

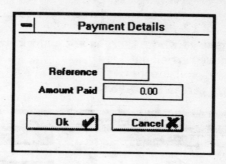

Details

This option enables you to add comments or to amend any of the displayed details. There is also (in v2.1) a CALCULATE NET button which works out the NET and VAT figures from the gross. Discounts can also be calculated.

Abandon / Close

ABANDON lets you clear the screen to enter the details again, CLOSE returns you to the previous screen.

To edit an invoice you have created, simply highlight it within the first INVOICING screen and then click on the INVOICE button, the invoice will be displayed and you can alter it.

Service

This option is used where there is not a stock item e.g. for a service you have carried out.

The data entry screen look like this.

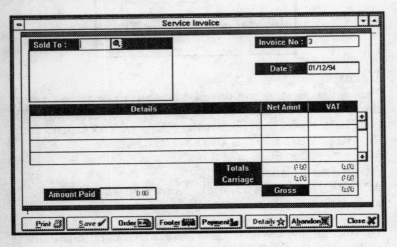

The rest of the invoice follows the same pattern as the INVOICE option dealt with above.

Credit Note

If you have stock items returned to you and you want to issue a credit note to your customer then select this option.

You can also enter non-stock items by using the codes shown below.

S1	Taxable non stock item
S2	Zero rated non stock item
M	Text only

The data entry screen is similar to the original stock one and you deal with it in the same way.

You should make sure the codes are the same as the original.

The stock records are also updated by using this option after using the UPDATE option.

Print Batch

If you have batched your invoices then you can select to print one or all of them by selecting this option.

Update

It is very important to do this as your ledgers will not be updated otherwise.

This is a useful option because it will tell you if you have not completed the invoice properly for example by not allocating a NOMINAL code to carriage and so on.

This process generates a report which will tell you if the invoice has not been posted and why, it is best to print this report and read it.

Note that you can only update an invoice to the ledger once.

Delete

You can delete any of the displayed invoices or credit notes by highlighting them and then selecting this button. You will be pleased to know that like most of the delete commands this contains a fail-safe where you will be asked to confirm the deletion.

However this is not a good idea once you have updated (posted) the ledgers. Deleting a posted invoice does **not** reverse the posting.

SOP - Sales Order Processing

This option lets you create sales orders for your customers, which you can then send to them.

The first screen of the SOP (sale order processing) is shown below.

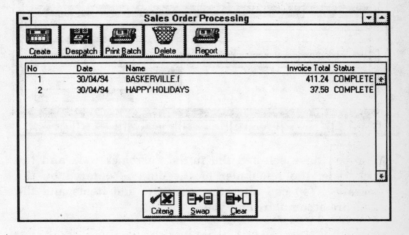

Create

Create

To create an order click on the CREATE button. The data entry screen will appear.

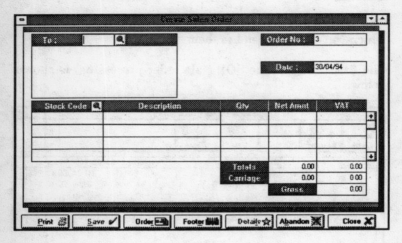

After you have selected the initial customer code and the stock code, the remainder of the data is entered by the program. You can alter the quantity, add items and the totals are accumulated for you.

Note that you can enter a NON-STOCK item by using any of the following codes in the STOCK CODE field. If you enter any of these an additional dialog box will appear into which you can enter details of the non stock item.

S1	Taxable non stock item
S2	Zero rated non stock item
M	Text only

At the bottom of the screen are various buttons, these are functionally the same as within the other options already dealt with.

The DETAILS screen is shown below.

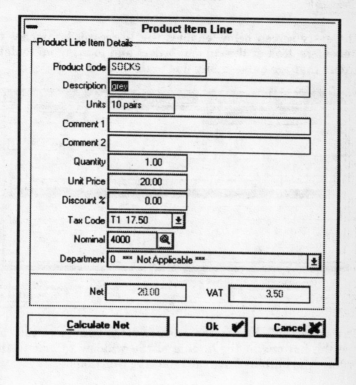

Despatch

Despatch

The entry screen below enables you to record despatches to
customers, look at the current orders and to bring up to date
orders that are outstanding due to the lack of stock.

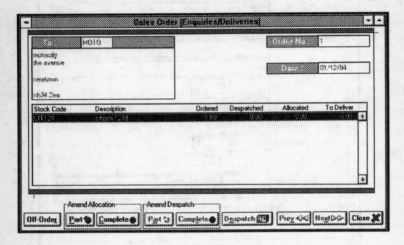

The screen will display the selected stock items and you can
use the buttons at the bottom of the window to amend the
order. The buttons have the following functions.

Off-Order

This can be changed from OFF-ORDER to ORDER (and
back) by clicking on it. If OFF-ORDER is shown then any
item can be highlighted and the allocation amended.

Amend Allocation (Part or Complete)

Part Allocation prompts you for the number of stock items to
allocate to the particular order and Complete Allocation
allocates all the required stock to complete the order.

Amend Despatch (Part or Complete)
As with the allocation you can amend the number despatched on this order.

You can only select to amend despatch after having allocated stock to this particular order.

Despatch
Click here to despatch the order (you can only do this after having allocated stock to the order).

Clicking on the DESPATCH button brings up another screen.

You can allocate the stock by clicking on the allocation button and despatch it in a similar way by clicking on the DESPATCH button which brings up the following screen.

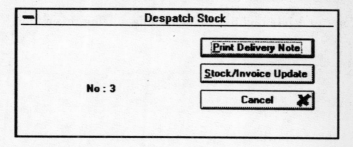

Print Delivery Note
Pretty self explanatory.

Stock / Invoice Update
This will update the stock and create an invoice record which you can post using the INVOICING option which was dealt with earlier.

Close
When you have finished and wish to return to the previous menu.

Print Batch

This prints off the (highlighted) sales orders that have been batched previously.

Delete

You can delete highlighted sales orders using this option.

Report

Report

Clicking on this button will produce the screen shown below.
This is very similar to the other reporting screens described
in other sections.

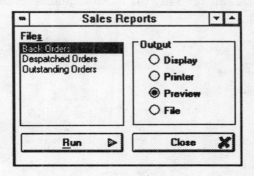

POP - Purchase Order Processing

This follows substantially the same sequence as Sales Order Processing.

Financials

Selecting this produces a set of icons dealing with the production of accounts, the initial screen is shown below.

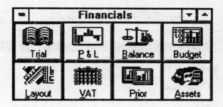

We will look at each of these in sequence starting with the Trial Balance.

Trial (Balance)

Trial

This lists the balances on the different nominal ledger accounts you have set up and entered data into, an example of the layout is shown below.

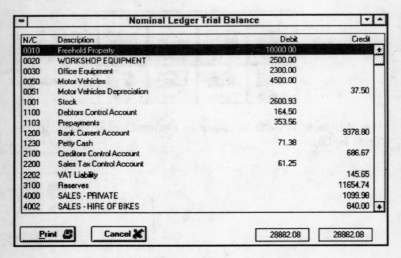

N/C	Description	Debit	Credit
0010	Freehold Property	10000.00	
0020	WORKSHOP EQUIPMENT	2500.00	
0030	Office Equipment	2300.00	
0050	Motor Vehicles	4500.00	
0051	Motor Vehicles Depreciation		37.50
1001	Stock	2600.93	
1100	Debtors Control Account	164.50	
1103	Prepayments	353.56	
1200	Bank Current Account		9378.80
1230	Petty Cash	71.38	
2100	Creditors Control Account		686.67
2200	Sales Tax Control Account	61.25	
2202	VAT Liability		145.65
3100	Reserves		11654.74
4000	SALES - PRIVATE		1099.98
4002	SALES - HIRE OF BIKES		840.00

Print   Cancel   28882.08   28882.08

There are two buttons at the bottom of this window allowing you to print the trial balance, or if you select CANCEL you will be returned to the previous menu.

P & L / Balance (Sheet)

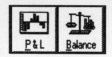

Clicking on either of these produces a dialog box which displays the current month. You can alter this to any month you wish.

You then have a choice of displaying the resulting set of accounts on the screen, you can print them (or preview them) either on the printer or to a file for future use.

The resulting display shows the selected month and the cumulative figures for the year to date.

Budget

This, again, produces a monthly report of the budget, the actual figures and the variance (difference between the actual and budgeted figures) for both the selected month and the year to date.

Layout

Layout

The dialog box that results from selecting this is shown below.

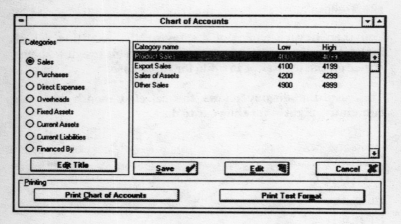

Firstly you can select a category and the relevant account codes within that category will be displayed on the right of the window. You can EDIT both the actual description of each code and the range of numbers applicable to that code by clicking on the EDIT buttons.

The buttons along the bottom of the window are:

Print Chart of Accounts
This is not as you may think a bar chart of the figures but a list of the account codes used. This list can be printed to file or the printer as well as displayed on the screen.

Print Test Format
Similar to the chart above only this time you get a list of the ranges rather than each individual code.

VAT Return

Calculate

You will need to click on the CALCULATE button to make the program look through the transactions for the period and produce a VAT return for you.

Check the figures against the Sales and Purchase Tax Control Accounts and if there is any discrepancy, you will need to find out why.

Reconcile

This sets a flag (or marker) to the items included within the current VAT return. This means that they will not be included again unless you want them to be by clicking on the INCLUDE RECONCILED TRANSACTIONS button.

The end result may look like this.

	Value Added Tax Return			
	SERIOUS CYCLES THE OLD SHED RAILWAY CUTTINGS BEDSTOW	Period from	01/04/94	
		to	30/04/94	

VAT due in this period on sales	**1**	133.94	
VAT due in this period on EC acquisitions	**2**	0.00	
Total VAT due (sum of boxes 1 and 2)	**3**	133.94	
VAT reclaimed in this period on purchases	**4**	240.64	
Net VAT to be paid to Customs or reclaimed by you	**5**	-106.70	
Total value of sales, excluding VAT	**6**	765.30	
Total value of purchases, excluding VAT	**7**	1375.07	
Total value of EC sales, excluding VAT	**8**	0.00	
Total value of EC purchases, excluding VAT	**9**	0.00	

☐ Include Reconciled Transactions

[Calculate ▦] [Reconcile ▦] [Print ▤] [Close ✗]

You can then look at the detailed breakdown of each figure
by clicking in the appropriate box and a screen showing the
breakdown will be displayed. A further breakdown can then
be displayed by selecting the appropriate button along the
bottom of that window.

It is suggested that you **zero** the tax control accounts at the
end of each month. This will mean that you are only dealing
with one month's figures at a time and will, therefore, find
the task of reconciling your figures easier.

To zero the tax codes simply find the balance on the
PURCHASE and SALES TAX CONTROL ACCOUNTS and
transfer the balances to the VAT LIABILITY ACCOUNT.

You must keep all your reports and work on the VAT return
and its reconciliation for inspection by the C&E.

Print

After selecting this you are given a choice as follows.

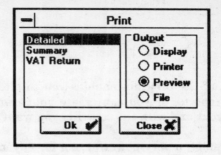

Close

To return to the previous screen.

Prior

This is similar to the BUDGET report described earlier, only this time the previous year's figures are included.

Assets

This displays the values of your assets, giving the original value, depreciation and current (book value) of each.

Reports

This section of the program enables you to alter or display
the default reports, or you can create your own reports, in
whatever layout and with the contents you want.

This is, therefore, a very powerful tool for anyone wanting a
specific report not catered for already.

The initial screen is shown below.

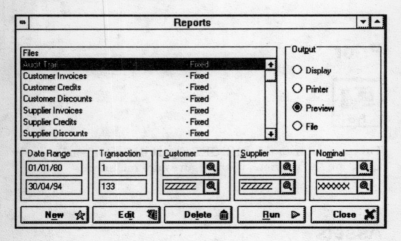

There are various boxes just above the buttons and these can
be left or they can be altered to the specific data you want to
enter (either by typing or clicking on the view symbol to the
right of the box and then selecting your choice(s)).

The buttons along the bottom of the window are as follows:

New
This lets you create your own report format within the entry screen shown below.

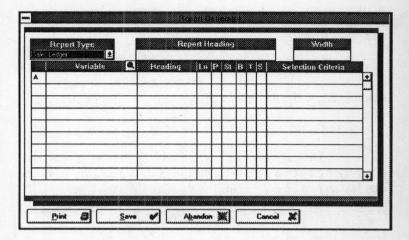

You can alter the Report Type and enter your chosen text in the Report Heading box, the Report Width box will be automatically filled as you enter each variable (a default width is automatically entered but you can change this).

Within the actual table each row is named with a letter, the first being given the letter **A** and when you get to it, the second will be named **B** and so on.

The **HEADING** is entered for you (and again you can alter this if you wish) as is the **Ln** column (this is short for length and defines the number of characters taken up by the specific variable).

P stands for print mode and you can select whether you want that specific field to be printed.

St is short for sort and you can choose the type of sorting (if any) you want within that field. The choices are specified by first the order of sorting and then Ascending or Descending. These are selected from within the VARIABLE dialog box as are the following items.

B stands for break and **L** or **P** a line break between columns or a page break.

T means totals or subtotals for this column of data, **Y** subtotals groups of data, **T** means only subtotals will be displayed not the individual figures.

S meaning sign, you enter a **D** for debit and so on.

The VARIABLE can be selected by clicking on the magnifying button and then on the chosen variable from the display as can be seen from the display shown.

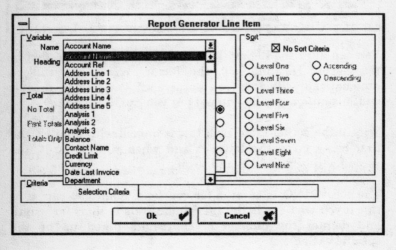

After selecting the Account Name you will see the following
screen which enables you to select the various options within
the report (as described above).

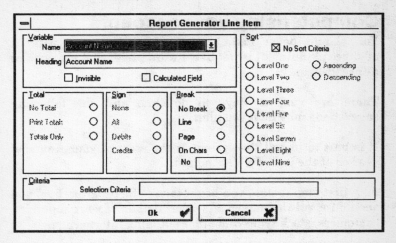

Selection Criteria shows the criteria you wanted to use
within this.

Edit
To change the layout of your report. You can only alter
reports you have created yourself.

Delete
You can delete any report you have created that you wish to
by using this option. You cannot delete the original fixed
reports.

Run
To actually display a report

Appendix one

Computerising your accounts

You should never install an accounting system without advance planning, it is not like a word processing program or a spreadsheet.

There are various ways to do this, and the following suggestions may help you plan.

It is best to install the system at the start of your financial year or at the end of a VAT period.

As a first step (before you begin to use the program live) you should install the names and other details of your suppliers, customers, stock types and other standing information.

One of the more difficult activities is setting up the Coding Structure. If you are unsure about this it is worth money to get a professional to help you. If you create a messy system it will be inefficient to use and costly to alter.

At the end of one accounting year and the beginning of the next extract the balances on all your accounts and then enter them into the new accounting system (obviously this will take a few days and may need your accountant's help).

Always run parallel systems for a period of time (this means running both the old manual and the new computerised systems side by side).

This is time consuming and costly but is a necessary security procedure if things go wrong. By checking the manual records against the computer versions you can clear up any misunderstandings and gain confidence at the same time.

Remember not to be too ambitious, it may be best to begin with the Sales Ledger and when this is working well, then to install the Purchase Ledger. By this time you will be more confident and may like to computerise the Nominal Ledger and Stock and so on.

Appendix two

Setting up SAGE for the first time

When you set up your accounting systems onto a computer for the first time there is a sequence of activities that are necessary to go through.

These are dealt with within this appendix.

Setting the financial year

Not all companies have the same financial year end so the first activity is to set the start of the financial year for your company. Click on the DEFAULTS command along the top of the window and then select FINANCIAL YEAR.

> You cannot alter this date once you have entered any data.

Enter details of your customers and suppliers

The next step is to enter the details of your existing customers and suppliers. Print out a list for reference purposes.

Enter the amounts due from customers and the amounts due to suppliers

These are best entered as individual balances for each invoice as they can more easily be allocated when payment is made and will also show up correctly analysed when displaying aged debtors or creditors reports.

Enter the date of the invoice (not the system date).

You can do this when creating the customer or supplier record by using the SETUP option within that screen. However SETUP does not provide any VAT analysis nor are the balances analysed to individual nominal accounts.

The normally recommended method is to enter the gross amount and use VAT code **T9** as the VAT should have been dealt with in previous VAT periods.

If you are using VAT CASH ACCOUNTING then you **must** enter them as individual transactions using the INVOICE (CREDIT NOTE) options within the CUSTOMERS or SUPPLIERS modules and entering the appropriate VAT codes. You must **not** use the SETUP options.

Deal with the Control Accounts

Entering the amount due to suppliers and from customers generates a balance on the SUSPENSE account and this will also appear on the Trial Balance when it is displayed.

These **must** be cleared BEFORE entering the list of ledger balances otherwise they will appear twice.

To display the Trial Balance (from the main menu) select FINANCIALS and then TRIAL and a list of the balances will appear.

WRITE THESE DOWN (there should only be three, the Debtors Control, the Creditors Control and the Suspense Account).

Before doing anything else it is necessary to remove these balances (the record of who owes money to whom will be retained).

To do this go back to the main menu and select NOMINAL, then JOURNALS. Enter the data in the opposite way to the way it is shown in the TRIAL BALANCE (remembering to alter the date if necessary).

Thus if it is a DEBIT balance in the TRIAL BALANCE then enter it as a CREDIT balance in the JOURNAL.

It is important to realise that you cannot SAVE a journal UNTIL it balances, in other words the total value of the debit column equals the total of the credit column. The results of the journal will be posted and the trial balance should have no values in it any more.

Close down the open windows and then display or print the TRIAL BALANCE **before** proceeding. Check there is no balance on the SUSPENSE account (A/C code 9998) or on any other account.

This is a once only operation.

Set Up the Nominal Ledger
Finally to finish the actual preparation work before you can enter the actual transactions, it is best to set up the NOMINAL codes to reflect your type of work by giving them the names you actually use in your business and (possibly) delete the ones you will not ever use.

Entering the opening trial balance
When you computerise your accounts you will need to enter the opening Trial Balance (the list of ledger balances that derive from the manual accounts you originally used).

Even if you are starting a new business, there will be opening balances to enter, for example the capital you are investing in the business.

To enter these balances, you select the N/C you want and then click on the SETUP button. This will display a dialog box that asks for the amount.

Please note that the date will be the system date (the date you are entering the data UNLESS you alter it to the date you actually want). I suggest that to avoid confusion you enter a date the day before the start of your accounting year. This means that the balance will show as the Brought Forward figure not as part of the first month's figure.

Click on TRIAL and check the figures carefully against the originals. There should be **no** SUSPENSE balance and the figures should be identical to those you entered.

If you make a mistake you can create a new journal entry to correct it.

You have successfully set up the ledger system now and are ready to begin to enter transaction data.

Stock
Now enter the stock records and their opening balances using the PRODUCTS module and within that the RECORD (and SETUP) button.

Then print out a product valuation to check that the data has been entered correctly (and that the stock figure agrees with the figure on the trial balance you entered earlier).

The dates entered within the stock module should be the first day of the accounting period.

Appendix three

Criteria

This lets you choose from all the records the specific ones you want. You do this by choosing certain criteria.

Selecting this brings up the dialog box shown below.

```
┌──────────────────────── Customer List Criteria ────────────────────────┐
│  ═│                                                                     │
│                                                                         │
│   Field          Criteria   Values            ┌─Balance Checks────────┐ │
│   [A/C]    □   [ = ]    [        ][        ]   │  ⦿ None               │ │
│   Name     □   [ = ]    [               ]     │  ○ Over Credit Limit  │ │
│   Street1  □   [ = ]    [               ]     │  ○ Balance Current    │ │
│   Street2  □   [ = ]    [               ]     │  ○ 30 - 60 Days       │ │
│   Town     □   [ = ]    [               ]     │  ○ 60 - 90 Days       │ │
│   County   □   [ = ]    [               ]     │  ○ 90 - 120 Days      │ │
│   Post Code □  [ = ]                          │  ○ Balance (Older)    │ │
│   Analysis1 □  [ = ]    [        ][        ]   └───────────────────────┘ │
│   Analysis2 □  [ = ]    [        ][        ]   ┌───────────────────────┐ │
│   Analysis3 □  [ = ]                          │   Criteria On  ✔✘     │ │
│   This Month □ [ = ]      0.00       0.00     │   Criteria Off ✔✘     │ │
│   YTD      □   [ = ]      0.00       0.00     │   Load          📁    │ │
│   Credit Limit □ [ = ]    0.00       0.00     │   Save          ✔     │ │
│   Balance  □   [ = ]      0.00       0.00     │   Delete        🗑     │ │
│                                               │   Abandon       ▨     │ │
└─────────────────────────────────────────────────────────────────────────┘
```

Field

You select a specific field by clicking on the box to the right of the field name so that a cross appear within the box, to deselect just click again so that the cross disappears.

Criteria

The criteria that can be used are :

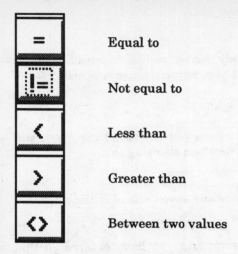

=   Equal to

!=   Not equal to

<   Less than

>   Greater than

<>   Between two values

You can switch between them by clicking on the symbol and it will change to the next in sequence.

Values

In the value boxes you can use letters or numbers and also various other characters e.g.

*   A wildcard signifying any character or characters e.g. =TR*
?   This stands for any one character e.g. =?D
$ Checks whether the specified text appears within the field, e.g. $money or $"fred fawcett" - if the text includes a space it must be included in inverted commas.

Balance Checks

Similarly with the Balance Checks clicking within the circle turns it on (a large dot will appear) and clicking again turns it off.

Criteria On / Off

This enables the criteria or disables them. They will still exist but will not affect the data.

Load

You can load an already saved set of criteria. This is obviously time saving if you regularly use a specific set of criteria.

Save

Once you have created criteria you can save them. You will be prompted for a filename when choosing this.

Delete

This enables you to remove any saved sets of criteria.

Abandon

Selecting this clears the criteria you have entered so that you can set new ones.

Appendix four

Transaction Types

Many of the reports and other screens identify transactions by type. Here is a list of the codes used in transactions.

SI / SC	Sales invoice / credit note
SR	Sales receipt
SA	Sales payment (on account)
SD	Sales discount
PI / PC	Purchase invoice / credit note
PP	Purchase payment
PA	Purchase payment (on account)
PD	Purchase discount
BP / BR	Bank payment / receipt
CP / CR	Cash payment / receipt
JD / JC	Journal debit / credit

The VAT column uses the following codes.

R	Reconciled
N	Unreconciled

There are also some codes specific to stock items and these are described below.

AI / AO	Adjustment in / out
MI / MO	Movement in / out (transfers only)
GR	Goods returned (credit notes)
GO	Goods out (SOP and INVOICING)
GI	Goods in (POP)

Appendix five

Previewing the reports

One of the new features of the program is being able to PREVIEW and alter the look of the data before printing it out.

At various points within the program you are given the opportunity to look at your data. You can then decide to print it, preview it (prior to printing it out), display it on screen or save it to a file.

Previewing lets you alter the fonts and font sizes of the data in various ways. The screen is shown below and this is followed by an explanation of each of the buttons.

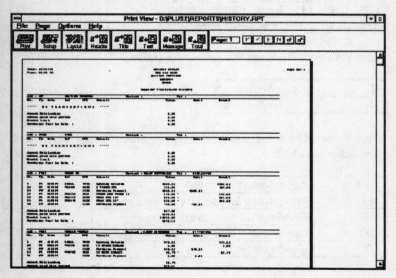

Print
This brings up the standard WINDOWS print dialog box.

Setup
Another standard WINDOWS dialog box which lets you alter various aspects of printing.

Layout
From this you can alter the margin measurements and switch between measuring in inches and centimetres.

Header / Title / Text / Message / Total
You can alter the font (typeface), the size of the type and the format (bold, italic, etc.) of the text.

Other Buttons
The small buttons to the right are paging (moving from one page to the next or backwards), scrolling (up and down) or zooming in or out (making the image bigger or smaller).

Some of these may be disabled if (for example) the text only fills a single page.

Appendix six

Stationery and report layouts

There are several layouts that come with the program. You can use these, you can alter them and save the altered version under a different name or you can create your very own customised layouts.

The following list shows the layouts that come with the program.

INVOICE.LYT	stock invoices/credit notes
INVTEXT.LYT	free text invoices
REMITT.LYT	remittance advices
STATMENT.LYT	statements
DESPATCH.LYT	despatch notes
SAORDER.LYT	sales orders
PUORDER.LYT	purchase orders
LABEL.SLB	customer labels
LABEL.PLB	supplier labels
OVERDUE.SAL	overdue letters
ADDRESS.PUR	change of address
FAX.SAL	customer faxes
FAX.PUR	supplier faxes

Appendix seven

The Convert Program (version 2.1)

This is installed for you in the SAGE program window and allows you to convert files from older versions of the program so that they can be used with v2.1.

The program must be used in conjunction with the instructions supplied by SAGE and, of course, you **must** take a backup of the original data **before** you attempt the conversion.

SAGE state that you must clear any Free Text Credit Notes if you are converting from Sterling version 6 (for DOS) as they will not be recognised by the new version.

The following screen will appear when you run the CONVERT program.

```
┌──────────────────────────────────────────────────┐
│ ▬|         Sage Convert v2.10                     │
│                                                    │
│   Select any of the following options:             │
│  ┌─Options─────────────────────────────────────┐  │
│  │  ☐ Convert Data                              │  │
│  │  ☐ Convert Layouts                           │  │
│  │                                              │  │
│  └──────────────────────────────────────────────┘  │
│                                                    │
│  ──────────────────────────────────────────────   │
│   Path to new program files                        │
│  ┌──────────────────────────────────────────────┐ │
│  │ D:\PLUS2                                       │ │
│  └──────────────────────────────────────────────┘ │
│                                                    │
│     ┌─────────┐  ┌──────────┐  ┌─────────┐         │
│     │ Browse  │  │ Continue │  │  Exit   │         │
│     └─────────┘  └──────────┘  └─────────┘         │
│                                                    │
└──────────────────────────────────────────────────┘
```

Appendix eight

Network Features of v2.1

Version 2.1 of the program is available in a network version and contains an automatic update feature for data.

For details of running the network version and the various update features and ways of maximising the speed of your network when running SAGE please refer to the documentation supplied by SAGE.

Index

G
Graphs, 73, 74

H
Help, 1, 3, 8, 9, 12, 34, 42, 43, 138

J
Journal, 71, 75, 76, 93, 94, 97, 141, 142, 143, 147

N
Nominal Codes, 3, 86, 90, 101, 114, 118

P
Parallel Systems, 12, 138
Password, 10, 11, 15, 18
Prepayments, 39, 76, 77
Preview, 62, 64, 93, 129, 148
Printer Setup, 15
Profit & Loss Account, 69

R
Recurring Entries, 94, 95
Restore, 32, 33, 34

S
Scroll Bars, 2
Security, 138
Spreadsheet, 138
Statements, 84, 85, 93
Suspense Account, 52, 68, 71, 141, 142, 143

T
Tax Codes, 23, 132
Trial Balance, 71, 127, 128, 141, 142, 143
Turnover, 54, 60

V
VAT Cash Accounting, 19, 20, 46, 47, 49, 141

Notes

Notes

Notes

Notes

Notes

Notes